Contents

Introduction

Words, words, words ...

When you learn a foreign language, you have to learn a lot of words. But of the many, many words in the English language (over half a million in all!), you really only need to know quite a small number. For every theme or subject, you will find there are 'key words' that help you to express what you want to say (and to understand what you hear and read). *Key Words in Context* contains this useful basic vocabulary.

But learning words can be boring. And, as every student knows, there are always words that are very difficult to remember! However, learning words is easier if you learn them in a *context* – together with other words and phrases that 'belong' to the same theme. *Key Words in Context* is divided into twelve chapters, each with its own theme. The texts and dialogues have been specially written to include the vocabulary you will need to know for each subject. Topics have been chosen which the various German states recommend for the 'Mittelstufe'.

How to work with Key Words in Context

- When you read the texts on the left-hand page, you will find you already know a number of the words. You will probably understand most of the others from the context. The German translation of each word (or phrase) is given on the right-hand page, as it fits the context. Related words are also sometimes given, many of which you will probably know.
  e.g. p. 15:
  rocky   rock   felsig   Fels, großer Stein

- Some words may be pronounced differently from how you would expect. To help you in these cases, the phonetics are given in brackets.
  e.g. p. 7
  continent ['kɒntɪnənt]   Kontinent

- Verbs with a star (*) in front of them are irregular. The forms are listed separately (see pages 148–149).
  e.g. p. 7
  to *be made up of   bestehen aus etwas

- Each chapter is complete in itself. So you needn't work through the book from beginning to end. Pick out the themes you need – when you need them.

- Don't try to learn too many words at once! 'Little and often' is more effective. Make sure you have the book with you at those times of the day when nothing is happening (when you're waiting for a bus, for example, or sitting on the train!).

- The more often you read a text or dialogue, the quicker you will learn the new vocabulary – and the more confidently you will be able to use it!

Features

This part of the book is to help you with other aspects of using vocabulary. It is arranged according to 'problem spots' rather than themes. It shows you, for example, how to express an opinion, how to write letters in English – and what phrases to use. A list of 'difficult' words that have several meanings is included. There is also a list of 'false friends' (words that look similar in English and German, but have different meanings). And there is a section which shows you how common verbs can be used as part of phrases and idioms. You will also find words that help to describe people – and feelings – in *Features,* and you can look up how to use those 'tricky' words that appear only in the singular or only in the plural.

The *Features* chapter will help you especially with your preparation for exams.

Geography

1 The continent of Europe

N W E S EUROPE

27

3 4 6 31

34 32 33 36 26

5

7 11 18

8 19 20 35

10 12 28 21 29

37 23 24a

22 24b 30

15 22 38

14 13 24b 35 16 17

Stand Dezember 1994

Europe is the world's second smallest continent. Most of its countries lie on the mainland of the continent. But over a third of its land is made up of islands and peninsulas, so a large number of Europeans live near the sea.

country	the people	adjective
Great Britain (1)	the British/Britons	British
Ireland (2)	the Irish	Irish
Norway (3)	the Norwegians [nɔːˈwiːdʒnz]	Norwegian
Sweden (4)	the Swedes	Swedish
Denmark (5)	the Danes	Danish
Finland (6)	the Finns	Finnish
the Netherlands (7)	the Dutch	Dutch
Belgium (8) [ˈbeldʒəm]	the Belgians	Belgian
Luxembourg (9)	the Luxembourgers	Luxembourgian
France (10)	the French	French
Germany (11)	the Germans	German
Switzerland (12)	the Swiss	Swiss
Spain (13)	the Spanish/Spaniards	Spanish
Portugal (14) [ˈpɔːtʃʊgl]	the Portuguese [ˌpɔːtʃʊˈgiːz]	Portuguese
Italy (15)	the Italians	Italian
Greece (16)	the Greeks	Greek
Turkey (17)	the Turks	Turkish
Poland (18)	the Poles	Polish
the Czech Republic (19)	the Czechs	Czech
Slovakia (20)	the Slovaks	Slovakian
Hungary (21)	the Hungarians	Hungarian
Bosnia-Herzegovina (22)	the Bosnians	Bosnian
Croatia (23) [krəʊˈeɪʃə]	the Croats	Croatian
Serbia (24 a) [sɜːbɪə]	the Serbs	Serbian
Montenegro (24 b) [ˌmɒntɪˈniːgrəʊ]	the Montenegrins	Montenegrin
Ukraine (26) [juːˈkreɪn]	the Ukrainians	Ukrainian
Iceland (27)	the Icelanders	Icelandic
Austria (28) [ˈɒstrɪə]	the Austrians	Austrian

Romania (29), Bulgaria (30), Russia (31), Latvia (32), Lithuania (33), Estonia (34), Moldavia (35), Byelorussia (36) [ˌbjeləʊˈrʌʃə], Slovenia (37), Macedonia (38) *und* Albania (39), *bilden das Wort für die Bevölkerung und das Adjektiv so wie Austria, d. h.* –ns, –n.

continent [ˈkɒntɪnənt]	Kontinent
Europe [ˈjʊərəp]	Europa
world	Welt
country	Land
mainland [ˈmeɪnlænd]	Festland
to *be made up of s.th.	bestehen aus etwas
island [ˈaɪlənd]	Insel
peninsula [pəˈnɪnsjʊlə]	Halbinsel
European [ˌjʊərəˈpiːən] *(noun/adj.)*	Europäer/in; europäisch
sea	Meer

2   The British Isles

The British Isles are made up of two large islands, Britain and Ireland – and a number of small islands around their coasts. Britain itself is divided into three parts: England, Scotland and Wales. Together, their official name is Great Britain.

The United Kingdom (often called the UK) includes Great Britain and Northern Ireland. The Republic of Ireland, which lies on the southern side of the border, is not part of the UK.

The North Sea lies on the eastern side of the British Isles; the Atlantic Ocean is on the western side. Britain is separated from the mainland of Europe by the English Channel.

Great Britain: natural resources and industries – old and new

England is the oldest industrialized country in the world. The invention of the steam engine in the 18th century marked the beginning of the Industrial Revolution. Machines could now do work that used to be done by hand. Coal was needed for the engines that drove the new machinery. So the Midlands and the North of England, where there is a lot of coal, soon developed into important industrial areas.

Manchester became the centre of the cotton industry, while Bradford and Leeds were famous for the wool trade. The raw materials were mainly imported from abroad. Special factories produced the finished textiles, which could then be exported.

> – Why do birds fly south in the winter?
> – Because it's too far to walk.

the British Isles [aɪlz]	die Britischen Inseln
Britain	Britannien
coast	Küste
to *be divided [dɪ'vaɪdɪd] into	geteilt sein in
the United [ju:'naɪtɪd] Kingdom	das Vereinigte Königreich
north, North	Norden, Nord-
northern (adj.)	nördlich
south, South	Süden, Süd-
southern (adj.)	südlich
east, East	Osten, Ost-
eastern (adj.)	östlich
west, West	Westen, West-
western (adj.)	westlich

Wenn **north, south, east, west** *Teil eines Eigennamens sind, werden sie groß geschrieben.*

Northern Ireland ['aɪələnd]	Nordirland
the Republic of Ireland	die Republik Irland
border	Grenze
to *be separated ['sepəreɪtɪd] from	getrennt sein von
the English Channel	der Ärmelkanal
natural resources [rɪ'sɔːsɪz]	Bodenschätze
industry	Industrie
industrialized country	Industrieland
invention [ɪn'venʃn]	Erfindung
steam engine ['endʒɪn]	Dampfmaschine
Industrial Revolution	Industrielle Revolution
by hand	mit der Hand/von Hand
coal	Kohle
machinery [mə'ʃiːnərɪ] (singular only)	Maschinen
to develop [dɪ'veləp]	(sich) entwickeln
industrial area ['eərɪə]	Industriegebiet, Industrieregion
cotton ['kɒtn]	Baumwolle
wool [wʊl]	Wolle
trade	Handel, Gewerbe
raw materials [mə'tɪərɪəlz]	Rohstoffe
to import [–'–]	importieren, einführen
(from) abroad [ə'brɔːd]	(aus dem) Ausland
to go abroad	ins Ausland gehen
factory	Fabrik
to produce	herstellen
textiles ['tekstaɪlz]	Textilien
to export [–'–]	exportieren, ausführen

Even today, Liverpool is still Europe's greatest Atlantic seaport, with seven miles of docks at the mouth of the Mersey. Manchester, also a vast urban area, is joined to the sea by the Manchester Ship Canal, and is an important inland port.

The development of the iron industry also began in the 18th century. Coal was needed for the mass production of iron. So, naturally, the iron and steel industry grew especially in areas where there was also coal-mining.

Britain's traditional industries include heavy engineering, ship-building and the chemical industry (especially in the North), the manufacturing of textiles, the car industry (especially in the Midlands), and the fishing industry (especially on the East coast). Some of these industries have declined now, and many pits, shipyards and works have had to close. Many cities have new industrial estates, where new companies – in modern industries such as plastics and electronics – have set up business. The demand for coal has declined; natural gas and North Sea oil have become more important – and, with them, the building of oil rigs, pipelines and refineries. The tourist industry and many different service industries also play an important role in present-day Britain.

Agriculture

The eastern part of England has very fertile soil, which makes good farmland. Wheat is one of the main crops. In southern England, there is a lot of dairy farming. Kent, in the South-East, is called the 'Garden of England', because of all the fruit and vegetables that are grown there.

seaport	Seehafen
docks	Hafenanlagen
mouth	Mündung
urban ['ɜːbən]	städtisch
to join	verbinden
canal [kə'næl]	Kanal
inland ['ınlənd] **port**	Binnenhafen
iron ['aıən]	Eisen
mass production	Massenproduktion
steel	Stahl
coal-mining	Kohlenbergbau
heavy engineering [ˌendʒı'nıərıŋ]	Schwerindustrie
shipbuilding	Schiffbau
chemical ['kemıkl]	chemisch, Chemie-
manufacturing [ˌmænjʊ'fæktʃərıŋ]	Herstellung, Fabrikation
car industry	Autoindustrie
to decline [dı'klaın]	in Verfall geraten, abfallen, nachlassen
pit	Zeche
shipyard ['ʃıpjɑːd]	(Schiffs-)Werft
works *(plural only)*	Werk
industrial estate	Industriegebiet, Gewerbegebiet
company ['kʌmpənı]	(Handels-)Gesellschaft, Firma
plastic	Kunststoff
electronics	Elektronik
to *set up business ['bıznıs]	sich niederlassen
business	Geschaft, Betrieb
demand [dı'mɑːnd]	Nachfrage
natural gas	Erdgas
oil rig	(Öl-)Bohrinsel
pipeline	(Rohr-)Leitung
refinery [rı'faınərı]	Raffinerie
service industry	Dienstleistungsbetrieb
agriculture ['æɡrıkʌltʃe]	Landwirtschaft
fertile ['fɜːtaıl]	fruchtbar
soil	Erde, Boden
farmland ['fɑːmlænd]	Ackerland
wheat [wiːt]	Weizen
crops	Feldfrüchte, Ernte
dairy ['deərı] **farming**	Milchwirtschaft
fruit [fruːt]	Obst
vegetables ['vedʒtəblz]	Gemüse

The moors that are so typical of the North of England, Scotland and Wales, are ideal for sheep farming.

Visitors to England are often fascinated by the hedges that divide the farmland into meadows and fields. Many of these hedges were planted in the eighteenth century, when big landowners divided their land into compact farms. But although the hedges are still there, British farms today are usually large – larger than farms in Germany, and often with more modern equipment.

Living conditions

Over 30% of Great Britain's population live in the South-East of England, many of them in London, which has been the capital for nearly 1,000 years. Central London is not an ideal place to live. The cost of living is high, the streets are crowded, and noise is a problem. Most people who work in the City of London are commuters: they live in quiet residential areas in the suburbs and travel to work by public transport.

Many of Britain's inner cities became uglier and shabbier when traditional industries declined. There is still a lot of poverty in some urban areas. But many of the old buildings have been pulled down, and new housing estates have now replaced a lot of the slums.

Living out in the country, where the air is fresh and clean, has become more and more popular – at least for people who can afford it. In Britain, not many of the people who live in rural districts actually work on the land.

North Sea oil and gas have brought big changes – and more wealth – to the inhabitants of many small towns and villages on the coast of Scotland and the Shetland Islands. Many local people who used to work as fishermen now work in jobs related to the oil industry.

moor(s)	Moor, Heidelandschaft
sheep *(plural: sheep)*	Schaf
hedge	Hecke
meadow [ˈmedəʊ]	Wiese
field	Feld, Acker
to plant [plɑːnt]	pflanzen
farm	Bauernhof
equipment [ɪˈkwɪpmənt] *(singular only)*	Ausstattung, Ausrüstung
living conditions	Lebensbedingungen
population [ˌpɒpjʊˈleɪʃn]	Bevölkerung
capital	Hauptstadt
place	Ort, Gebiet
cost of living to cost	Lebenshaltungskosten kosten
crowded	überfüllt
noise	Lärm
the City of London	das Banken- und Börsenviertel Londons
city	Großstadt
commuter [kəˈmjuːtə]	Pendler/in
residential area [ˌrezɪˈdenʃlˈeərɪə]	(vornehmes) Wohngebiet
suburb [ˈsʌbɜːb]	Vorort
public transport	öffentliche Verkehrsmittel
inner city	Innenstadt
ugly [ˈʌglɪ]	hässlich
shabby [ˈʃæbɪ]	schäbig, heruntergekommen
poverty [ˈpɒvətɪ]	Armut
building	Gebäude, Haus
to pull s.th. down	etwas niederreißen
housing estate	Wohnsiedlung
slum [slʌm]	Elendsviertel
in the country	auf dem Land
air	Luft
to afford [əˈfɔːd] s.th.	sich etwas leisten
rural [ˈrʊərəl]	ländlich
district	Bezirk, Gegend
to work on the land	in der Landwirtschaft arbeiten
wealth [welθ]	Wohlstand, Reichtum
inhabitant [ɪnˈhæbɪtənt]	Einwohner/in
village [ˈvɪlɪdʒ]	Dorf
local [ˈləʊkl]	örtlich, hiesig

3   The United States of America

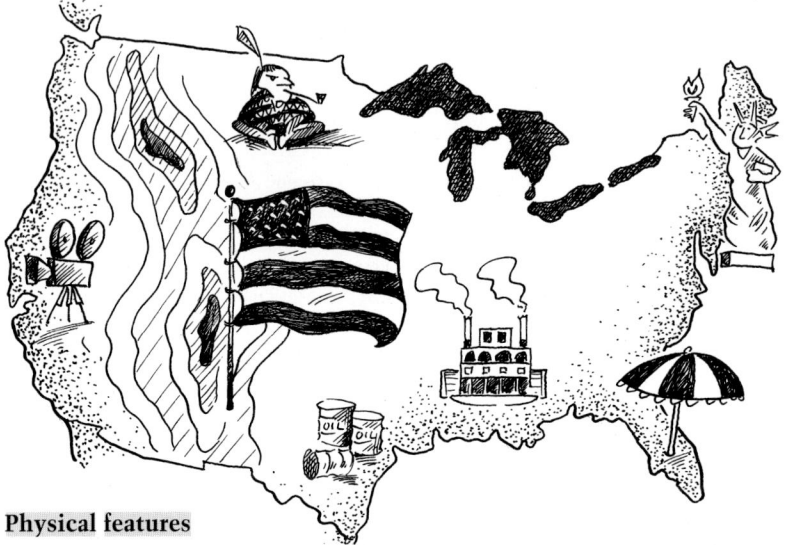

Physical features

The USA is an enormous country. The first thing about America that
amazes visitors is, in fact, its size. The distance across the USA from
coast to coast is three thousand miles; from the Canadian border in the
north to the Gulf of Mexico in the south, it is twelve hundred miles.
The country has an area of 9.3 million square kilometres (to compare:
the European Community countries have only 2 million).

Geographically, the USA has three dominant features: the two long
mountain ranges on each side of the country (the Appalachians in the
east and the Rocky Mountains in the west), and the wide valley
between them, with its huge prairie which rises to the Great Plains,
and with its large rivers which flow into the great Mississippi.

Visitors are always impressed by the beauty of the landscape. The
scenery in the west is especially dramatic, with its many types of landscape and climate. California has a long coastline, rocky in places, with
miles of sandy beaches and lovely bays. Further inland, there is the
mountainous region of the Sierra Nevada (the summit of Mount Whit-
ney is 4,418 metres above sea-level). Not far away is the wilderness of
endless desert that surrounds Death Valley, the lowest point in the
USA (86 metres below sea-level). The ground here is very dry and stony.
There are also vast National Parks with beautiful forests, rivers and
streams; and there are miles of wooded countryside.

physical	physikalisch, landschaftlich, geographisch
feature ['fiːtʃə]	Merkmal, Besonderheit
enormous [ɪ'nɔːməs]	riesig
size	Größe
distance ['dɪstəns]	Entfernung
mile	Meile
area ['eərɪə]	*hier:* Fläche
square kilometre	Quadratkilometer
mountain range	Bergkette
wide width	breit, weit Breite
valley	Tal
huge [hjuːdʒ]	gewaltig, riesig
prairie ['preərɪ]	Prärie (Grasebene)
plain	Ebene
river	Fluss, Strom
to flow [fləʊ]	fließen
landscape	Landschaft
scenery ['siːnərɪ]	Szenerie, Landschaft
climate ['klaɪmɪt]	Klima
coastline	Küstenlinie
rocky rock	felsig Fels, großer Stein
sandy sand	sandig Sand
beach	Strand
bay	Bucht
inland ['ɪnlænd]	im Landesinneren
mountainous ['maʊntɪnəs]	gebirgig
summit	Gipfel
above/below sea-level	über/unter dem Meeresspiegel
wilderness ['wɪldənɪs]	Wildnis
desert ['dezət]	Wüste
to surround [sə'raʊnd]	umgeben
low	niedrig
ground	Boden
stony stone	steinig Stein
vast [vɑːst]	sehr groß und weitläufig
National Park	Nationalpark
forest	Wald
stream [striːm]	Bach
wooded ['wʊdɪd] wood	bewaldet Wald
countryside	Land(schaft)

Up in the hills, dams have been built to create reservoirs, which supply water for the cities and for the fields and gardens of southern California.

When the American glaciers melted about 5,000 years ago, the Great Lakes were formed. Some of the wildest countryside on the North American continent is to be found in this area – although there are also large cities, like Chicago and Detroit, on the shores of the lakes. Between two of the lakes, the Niagara Falls, America's most spectacular waterfall, forms a natural border between the USA and Canada.

The states of Kansas, Iowa and Nebraska, in the heart of the USA, are largely flat, with huge expanses of farmland. The great open spaces of the Midwest and the South are ideal for cattle ranches. Florida, in the southeast, is also flat. With its mild climate, it is famous for the seaside resorts along its coastline – and for the Everglades, a wilderness of swampland near Miami.

The forces of nature

Disasters caused by the forces of nature are not uncommon in the USA. There are a number of active volcanoes near the West Coast; sometimes serious eruptions occur. The area around San Francisco is often affected by earthquakes.

Hurricanes sometimes create chaos in coastal areas, especially in the south and east, while tornadoes are whirlwinds that cause damage especially in inland areas. In the winter months, there are often blizzards that sweep down the country from the north.

hill	Hügel
dam	Damm
reservoir	Reservoir, Talsperre
to supply [sə'plaɪ]	*hier:* liefern
glacier ['glæsjə]	Gletscher
to melt	schmelzen
lake	(der) See
wild [waɪld]	wild
shore [ʃɔː]	Ufer, Strand
waterfall	Wasserfall
heart [hɑːt]	Herz, Mitte
flat	flach
expanse [ɪk'spæns]	*hier:* weiter Raum, Fläche
cattle ranch [rɑːntʃ]	Viehfarm
mild [maɪld]	mild
seaside resort [rɪ'zɔːt]	Seebad, Ferienort am Meer
swampland ['swɒmplænd]	Sumpfgebiet
forces of nature	Naturgewalten
disaster [dɪ'zɑːstə]	Katastrophe
active	aktiv, tätig
volcano [vɒl'keɪnəʊ]	Vulkan
eruption [ɪ'rʌpʃn]	Ausbruch
to erupt	ausbrechen
to affect	betreffen
earthquake ['ɜːθkweɪk]	Erdbeben
hurricane ['hʌrɪkən]	Orkan
tornado [tɔ'neɪdəʊ]	Wirbelsturm, Tornado
whirlwind ['wɜːlwɪnd]	Wirbelwind
damage ['dæmɪdʒ]	Schaden
blizzard ['blɪzəd]	heftiger Schneesturm
to *sweep	fegen

The USA – a country of superlatives

Here are just a few of the world records held by the United States.
It has …

● the most extensive cave system in the world: under the ground at
the Mammoth Cave National Park in Kentucky. So far, over 300 miles
of underground passageways have been discovered and mapped.
Mammoth Cave itself has five different levels. The lowest level is
110 metres below the surface.

● the world's highest mountain (measured from its base under the sea):
Mauna Kea in Hawaii, which is 10,023 metres high (4,205 metres of
this height is above sea-level).

● the largest freshwater lake in the world: Lake Superior, with a total
area of 31,800 square miles.

● the largest gorge in the world: the Grand Canyon in Arizona. It
stretches over a distance of 217 miles, is between 4 and 13 miles wide,
and 1,615 metres deep.

● the highest cliffs: near Umilehi Point in Hawaii. They stand 1,005
metres above the sea.

● the world's greatest tides: in the Bay of Fundy between the USA
and Canada. The difference between high and low tide can be over
16 metres.

● the most enormous tree in the world: 'General Sherman', a giant
sequoia tree in the Sequoia National Park, California. This tree would
give enough wood to produce 5,000,000,000 matches.

● the world's largest flowering plant: a giant Chinese wisteria at
Sierra Madre, California. When in flower, it is covered in one and a half
million blossoms.

● the steepest streets in the world: in San Francisco, with gradients
up to 31.5%. In parts, the slopes are so extreme that cars have to park
with their front wheels turned inwards.

extensive [ɪk'stensɪv]	ausgedehnt, umfangreich
cave [keɪv]	Höhle
passageway ['pæsɪdʒ,weɪ]	Gang
to discover	entdecken
discovery	Entdeckung
to map	kartographisch darstellen
map	Landkarte
level	Ebene, Schicht, Etage
surface ['sɜːfɪs]	Oberfläche
to measure ['meʒə]	messen
measurement	Maß
base	Basis, Fuß
height [haɪt]	Höhe
freshwater	Süßwasser
gorge [gɔːdʒ]	Schlucht
to stretch [stretʃ]	sich erstrecken
deep	tief
cliff	Klippe, Felsen
tide [taɪd]	Ebbe und Flut
high tide	Flut
low tide	Ebbe
wood [wʊd]	*hier:* Holz
flowering	blühend
to flower	blühen
plant	Pflanze
in flower	in Blüte
flower	Blume
blossom ['blɒsəm]	Blüte, einzelne Blume
steep	steil
gradient ['greɪdjənt]	Steigung
slope	Hang, Neigung

4   The weather forecast

TV weatherman:
And now for tomorrow's weather. London and the South-East will have a bright start to the day, with plenty of sunshine. But it will become cloudy later, with outbreaks of rain or drizzle in some areas.

The South-West and the Channel Islands will have an unsettled day. There will be sea mist in many coastal areas in the morning, and there may be some heavy rain with high winds later in the day.

In the Midlands, Wales, Northern Ireland and the North of England, it will be mainly dry. It will be rather dull at first, and there may be patches of fog in some places. But there will be brighter weather, with some sunny spells, in most districts during the afternoon.

Most of Scotland will have another cool day, with a strong breeze, especially along the East coast. There may be a few scattered showers in the West.

Temperatures in most parts will be similar to today's. Around 8 to 10 degrees centigrade – milder in the South-West.

The outlook for the next few days: Colder weather will spread across the country from the North-East, and temperatures may fall below freezing point in some areas. There may even be the odd fall of snow or sleet on the Scottish hills, with danger of icy roads.

Holiday weather

Harry: Great to see you, Joe! How was Spain?

Joe: Fantastic, Harry. Except for the weather.

Harry: Oh?

Joe: It was good the first day or two. Not a cloud in the sky. Really hot. Then one evening we had a terrible storm. You know – thunder and lightning – and it poured! After an hour or so, the streets were all flooded, so we couldn't leave our hotel. A tree outside the hotel was blown down in the gale, so the road was blocked. But we were lucky. The hotel opposite ours was struck by lightning!
– Well, the weather never really cleared up properly after that. It wasn't warm enough to go swimming. And the sea was too rough anyway – the waves were enormous.

weather forecast ['fɔːkɑːst]	Wettervorhersage
weatherman	Meteorologe, 'Wetterfrosch'
a bright start to the day	freundliches Wetter in der Früh
cloudy	wolkig, bewölkt
outbreaks of rain	Regenperioden
drizzle ['drɪzl]	Nieselregen
unsettled [ˌʌn'setld]	unbeständig
sea mist	feiner Nebel vom Meer
heavy rain	starker Regen
high wind	starker Wind
dull	trüb, bewölkt
patches ['pætʃɪz] **of fog**	Nebelfelder
sunny spells	sonnige Abschnitte
strong breeze [briːz]	starke Brise
scattered showers	vereinzelte Schauer
degree (centigrade)	Grad (Celsius)
the outlook	die Aussichten
to *spread across the country	sich über das Land ausdehnen/ ausbreiten
below/above freezing point	unter/über Null
to freeze	frieren
the odd fall of snow	einzelne Schneefälle
sleet	Schneeregen
not a cloud in the sky	keine Wolke am Himmel
storm	Gewitter
thunder	Donner
lightning	Blitz
to pour [pɔː]	gießen
flooded ['flʌdɪd] flood	überflutet Überschwemmung
gale [geɪl]	starker Wind
to *be struck by lightning	vom Blitz getroffen werden
to clear up	(sich) aufklären
rough [rʌf]	rauh, stürmisch
wave	Welle

Did you hear about the boy who came to school with only one glove on? Well, the teacher asked him why. And he said, "The weather forecast said it might be warm, but on the other hand it might get quite cool."

Harry: Bad luck! – We had great weather here. A real heatwave. It got
so muggy at times, you could only sit outside if you were in the
shade. There hasn't been a wet day for weeks – we've had a real
drought.

Joe: Until today. Look at it – what a downpour! It's starting to hail
now, too. See the hailstones?

Harry: And the rainbow! That's the English climate for you. Full of
surprises. Just like Spain!

5   Looking at the sky at night

During the day, before the sun has set, it is easy to imagine that our
Earth is the centre of the universe. But at night, when it gets dark and
the moon rises, the sight of the millions of stars and planets in the sky
can make us feel very small.

Does life exist anywhere else in the universe? We know there can be
no other intelligent life in our own solar system. But could there be life
on any planets of other suns in outer space, perhaps in other galaxies?
These planets are so far away, of course, that nobody could ever make
the journey there. The distances to stars in the Milky Way are so enormous that they have to be measured in light years. (A light year is the
distance that light travels in one year – at a speed of about 660 million
miles an hour!)

> *– What did the man from outer space say to the petrol pump?*
> *– Take your finger out of your ear when I'm talking to you.*

Light and darkness

As everyone knows, the changing position of the globe as it moves
round the sun causes the changing seasons. In the winter, it is dark all
day and all night at the North Pole; but in the summer, the sun never
sinks below the horizon at all. When autumn comes to the northern
hemisphere, it is spring in the countries south of the equator.

So what must the seasons be like on Pluto, the most distant planet
in our solar system? Pluto takes nearly 250 years to go all the way
round the sun!

heatwave	Hitzewelle
muggy ['mʌgɪ]	schwül
in the shade	im Schatten
a wet day	ein Regentag
drought [draʊt]	Trockenperiode, Dürre
What a downpour! ['daʊnpɔ:]	Was für ein Wolkenbruch!
to hail [heɪl]	hageln
hailstone	Hagelkorn
rainbow ['reɪnbəʊ]	Regenbogen
during the day	am Tag
the sun *sets	die Sonne geht unter
our Earth	unsere Erde
earth	Erdboden, Erde
universe ['ju:nɪvɜ:s]	Universum
at night	nachts, in der Nacht
to *get dark	dunkel werden
the moon *rises	der Mond geht auf
sight	Anblick
star	Stern
planet ['plænɪt]	Planet
to exist	existieren, bestehen
solar ['səʊlə] **system**	Sonnensystem
outer ['aʊtə] **space**	Weltraum, Weltall
galaxy	Galaxie
the Milky Way	die Milchstraße
globe	Globus, die Erde
season ['si:zn]	Jahreszeit
all day	den ganzen Tag
all night	die ganze Nacht
the North Pole	der Nordpol
to *sink	untergehen, sinken
horizon [hə'raɪzn]	Horizont
autumn ['ɔ:təm]	Herbst
hemisphere ['hemɪˌsfɪə]	Halbkugel
spring	Frühling
equator [ɪ'kweɪtə]	Äquator
distant	weit entfernt

History

Some important periods and events – from prehistoric times to the present day

12,000 BC	The end of the Ice Age in Northern Europe
800–500 BC	The Iron Age: the Celts come to Britain
55 BC	The Romans first arrive in Britain
5th–9th century AD	The Angles and Saxons, then the Vikings, invade Britain
1066	The Norman conquest
11th–13th century	The Crusades: Christian armies from Europe go to the Holy Land
1215	King John signs Magna Carta
1265	The first Parliament (a meeting of knights, barons and townspeople) comes together in England
14th century	A plague, known as the Black Death, sweeps through Europe and kills half the population
1492	Christopher Columbus's first voyage to America
16th century	The Tudor Age: Henry VIII founds the Church of England; England becomes a sea power; for the next 300 years the British Navy is the strongest in the world
1689	The Bill of Rights is passed: no English monarch may rule without Parliament
1775	The American War of Independence begins
1789	The French Revolution
1805–1815	The Napoleonic Wars in Europe
1861–1865	The American Civil War
1837–1901	The age of Queen Victoria: a time of many reforms, inventions and great material progress
1914–1918	The First World War
1939–1945	The Second World War
1990	The reunification of Germany The end of the Cold War

– *What sort of music did people in the Stone Age like best?*
– *Rock music.*

period ['pɪərɪəd]	Zeitalter, Periode
event [–'–]	Ereignis
prehistoric [ˌpriːhɪ'stɒrɪk]	vorgeschichtlich
the present day	zum heutigen Tag
BC (= **before Christ**)	vor Christus
Ice Age	Eiszeit
Stone Age, Bronze [brɒnz] Age	Steinzeit, Bronzezeit
Iron ['aɪən] **Age**	Eisenzeit
the Celts [kelts]	die Kelten
the Romans	die Römer
century ['sentʃʊrɪ]	Jahrhundert
AD (= **anno Domini**)	nach Christus
the Angles ['æŋglz] **and Saxons**	die Angeln und Sachsen
the Vikings ['vaɪkɪŋz]	die Wikinger
to invade [–'–]	einmarschieren in
the Norman conquest ['kɒŋkwest]	die normannische Eroberung
the Crusades	Kreuzzüge
army ['ɑːmɪ]	Armee
king	König
to sign	unterzeichnen
Parliament ['pɑːləmənt]	Parlament
knight [naɪt]	Ritter
baron ['bærən] baroness	Baron Baronin
plague [pleɪg]	Pest
to kill	töten
voyage ['vɔɪdʒ]	Seereise
to found	gründen
the Church of England	die anglikanische Kirche
sea power	Seemacht
navy ['neɪvɪ]	(Kriegs-)Marine
monarch ['mɒnək]	Monarch/in
to rule	regieren, herrschen
War of Independence	Unabhängigkeitskrieg
revolution [ˌrevə'luːʃn]	Revolution
the (American) Civil ['sɪvl] **War**	der (US) Bürgerkrieg
queen	Königin
reform [rɪ'fɔːm]	Reform
invention [–'– –]	Erfindung
progress (singular only)	Fortschritt(e)
the First/Second World War	der Erste/Zweite Weltkrieg
reunification [ˌ– – – – –'– – –]	Wiedervereinigung
the Cold War	der Kalte Krieg

1   **Historic** events ... in Britain ...

Hastings

1066 is one of the most important dates in Britain's history. It was the year when England was invaded for the last time.

When King Edward I died in the spring of 1066, he left no son to succeed him. Harold, an English nobleman, was chosen by the English as his successor. But two other men also had a claim to the throne. One was the King of Norway. The other was the Duke of Normandy. As Harold would not give up his kingdom, Duke William and the Normans decided to attack. The King of Norway also made plans to fight for the English throne, so Harold was threatened by two enemies at the same time.

The Normans made preparations to conquer England. They built 800 ships and filled them with stores, with weapons, and with horses. They also loaded the ships with parts of wooden forts, which they planned to put together after the invasion.

In September, while William was waiting for the right wind to take his ships across the Channel, the King of Norway landed with his men in the North of England. Harold's army marched north to defend the country against the invaders. They defeated the Norwegians at the Battle of Stamford Bridge. But the battle was hard, and many soldiers lost their lives.

Harold and his men were resting at York when news reached them that William of Normandy had landed on the Sussex coast.

After a ten-day march, the English army arrived exhausted at Hastings, where the Norman soldiers had camped.

Next morning, on October 14th, the Normans attacked. Their soldiers were armed mainly with bows and arrows. The English fought mainly with battle-axes, although swords and shields were used by both sides. The battle was long and bloody, and many men were killed or wounded.

historic	historisch
date	Datum, Zeitpunkt
to die death	sterben Tod
to succeed s.o.	jdm nachfolgen
nobleman noblewoman	Adliger Adlige
successor	Nachfolger/in
claim (to)	Anspruch (auf)
throne [θrəʊn]	Thron
duke duchess [ˈdʌtʃɪs]	Herzog Herzogin
kingdom	Königreich
to attack	angreifen
to *fight (for)	kämpfen (um)
to threaten [ˈθretn]	(be)drohen
enemy	Feind/in
to conquer [ˈkɒŋkə]	erobern
stores	Vorräte
weapon [ˈwepən]	Waffe
fort	Fort, Festung
invasion [ɪnˈveɪʒn]	Invasion
to land	landen
to march [mɑːtʃ]	marschieren
to defend [dɪˈfend]	verteidigen
invader [ɪnˈveɪdə]	Eindringling
to defeat [dɪˈfiːt]	besiegen
battle	Schlacht
soldier [ˈsəʊldʒə]	Soldat/in
to *lose [luːz] **one's life**	ums Leben kommen
exhausted [ɪgˈzɔːstɪd]	erschöpft
to camp	*hier:* das Lager aufstellen
to *be armed	bewaffnet sein
bow [bəʊ]	Bogen
arrow	Pfeil
battle-axe	Streitaxt
sword [sɔːd]	Schwert
shield [ʃiːld]	Schild
bloody	blutig
to wound [wuːnd]	verwunden

In the end, luck was on the Normans' side: Harold was killed – shot in the eye by an arrow. When the English saw that their leader was dead and the battle lost, they gave up. Many of the soldiers fled, leaving their king dead on the battlefield.

So William had won the day. He marched with his men to London, where he was crowned King in Westminster Abbey on Christmas Day 1066.

But the victory at Hastings was only the beginning of William's conquest. For a long time the English people feared and hated the Normans. Over the next four years, revolts broke out all over the country. But they were not organized, so William was able to put them down and restore the peace. He gave the English noblemen's estates to Norman barons. He established his power by building hundreds of castles and forts all over England. (The most famous of these is the Tower of London.) William treated the people fairly when they obeyed him. But he could also be very cruel. In the North, he punished the people's rebellion simply by destroying everything. His men burned the crops, slaughtered the cattle, set fire to the houses and farms.

So the defeat was complete. The English ruling class was wiped out, and the country was ruled by a powerful French-speaking aristocracy.

Teacher: *What does Hastings 1066 mean to you?*
Pupil: *William the Conqueror's telephone number, sir.*

to *shoot	(er)schießen, treffen
leader to lead	Anführer/in, Führer/in führen
dead	tot
to *lose	verlieren
to *give up	aufgeben
to *flee	fliehen
battlefield	Schlachtfeld
to *win the day	den Kampf gewinnen
to crown [kraʊn] s.o.	jdn krönen
victory ['vɪktərɪ]	Sieg
people	hier: Volk
to fear [fɪə]	fürchten
to hate	hassen
hatred ['heɪtrɪd]	Hass
revolt [–'–]	Aufstand, Aufruhr
to *break out	ausbrechen
to *put down (a revolt)	(einen Aufstand) niederschlagen
to restore [–'–]	wiederherstellen
peace	Frieden
estate [ɪ'steɪt]	Landgut
to establish [ɪ'stæblɪʃ]	aufbauen, festigen
power	Macht
castle	Burg
to treat	behandeln
to obey [–'–]	gehorchen
cruel [krʊəl]	grausam
to punish ['pʌnɪʃ]	bestrafen
punishment	Strafe
rebellion [rɪ'beljən]	Rebellion, Aufstand
to destroy [dɪ'strɔɪ]	zerstören
destruction	Zerstörung
to *burn	verbrennen
to slaughter ['slɔːtə]	schlachten
to *set fire to s.th.	etwas in Brand setzen
defeat	Niederlage
ruling class	Oberschicht
to wipe [waɪp] out	völlig vernichten
powerful	mächtig
aristocracy [ˌærɪ'stɒkrəsɪ]	Adel, Elite

The **Gunpowder** Plot

When James I became King of England in 1603, England was officially a Protestant country. In those days, religion was the most important thing in many people's lives. At first, James was tolerant of the Catholics in England, but this made Parliament angry, so the laws against Catholics were made stricter again. In frustration, a group of Catholic fanatics made a plan to blow up the king and the Houses of Parliament on November 5th, 1605. But the plot was discovered, and Guy Fawkes, one of the leaders, was arrested. Later he was tortured and then executed for high treason.

(See Public holidays and festivities p. 110 for details of 'Guy Fawkes Night' in England today.)

The **execution** of Charles I

James's son, Charles I, came to the throne in 1625. He believed in the 'Divine Right of Kings': that is, God had chosen him to be king, so he had the right to rule the country without the help of Parliament – which he did for eleven years. Then he called Parliament to raise money for a war. But Parliament protested, and tried to limit the King's power. The quarrel between King and Parliament finally led to civil war. After years of fighting, King Charles was defeated and taken prisoner. He was brought to trial and condemned to death.

The execution took place in front of Whitehall Palace in London, on January 30th, 1649. It was the first time – and the last – that an English monarch was tried and condemned by his own subjects.

Oliver Cromwell, a member of Parliament and the leader of the army that had opposed the King, ruled the country until his death in 1658. Although Cromwell served his country well in some ways, he was a dictator. His followers, the Puritans, had very strict religious beliefs, and laws were made against games, dancing and even singing. So most English people were pleased when Parliament asked Charles's son to return from exile after Cromwell's death. So Charles II inherited the throne, and kings and queens have reigned over England ever since.

gunpowder	Schießpulver
plot	Verschwörung
Protestant ['– – –] *(adj./noun)*	protestantisch; Protestant/in
in those days	damals
religion [rɪ'lɪdʒən]	Religion
tolerant ['tɒlərənt]	tolerant
Catholic ['kæθlɪk] *(adj./noun)*	katholisch; Katholik/in
fanatic [fə'nætɪk]	Fanatiker/in
to *blow up	in die Luft sprengen
the Houses of Parliament	Tagungsort des brit. Parlaments
to discover	entdecken
discovery	Entdeckung
to arrest [ə'rest] **s.o.**	jdn verhaften
to torture ['tɔːtʃə] **s.o.**	jdn quälen, foltern
to execute ['– – –]	hinrichten
high treason ['triːzn]	Hochverrat
execution [ˌ– –'– –]	Hinrichtung
to *come to the throne [θrəʊn]	den Thron besteigen
to believe in s.th.	an etwas glauben
to raise money	Geld aufbringen
to protest [prə'test] **(against s.th.)**	(gegen etwas) protestieren
quarrel ['kwɒrəl]	Streit
to *take s.o. prisoner	jdn gefangennehmen
to *bring s.o. to trial	jdn vor Gericht bringen
to condemn s.o. to death	jdn zum Tode verurteilen
to *take place	stattfinden
palace	Palast
to try s.o.	jdn vor Gericht stellen
subject	*hier:* Untertan/in
to oppose	bekämpfen, Widerstand leisten gegen
to serve one's country	seinem Land dienen
dictator [dɪk'teɪtə]	Diktator/in
follower	Anhänger/in
religious belief	religiöser Glaube
to *make a law	*hier:* ein Gesetz verabschieden
exile ['eksaɪl]	Verbannung, Exil
to inherit s.th.	etwas erben
to reign [reɪn] **(over)**	(als Monarch/in) regieren, herrschen

2   Historic events ... in America

New beginnings – in a 'New World'

Virginia, the first British colony in America, was founded in 1607. Thirteen years later, the 'Pilgrims', who sailed over on the "Mayflower", settled further north and established their own democratic community. Many of them were Puritan refugees who had left Britain in search of religious freedom. Countless settlers in the years that followed were immigrants escaping from religious persecution in their home countries. Others – like many of the Irish who emigrated in the 19th century – were driven from home by famine.

How the colonies won their independence

By the middle of the 18th century, there were 13 British colonies on the East coast. Many of the colonists were angry because they were not represented in the British Parliament in London. When the British government decided on new taxes for the colonists, the colonists resisted. The War of Independence began. Britain and America were at war until 1783. But the Declaration of Independence was signed before that: on July 4th 1776, representatives of the 13 States signed this historic document.

Opening up the West

After Independence, people began to move westward. More and more immigrants were arriving in the East, so it was natural to want to explore the unknown territory further inland. People were prepared to suffer hardship at first, in the hope of building a better life. In the 1830s and 1840s, thousands of people were on the move, and the frontier (wherever civilization came to an end and the wilderness began) was pushed further and further to the West.

colony ['– – –]	Kolonie
pilgrim	Pilger/in
to settle	sich niederlassen, sich ansiedeln
community [kə'mju:nətɪ]	Gemeinschaft
refugee [ˌrefjʊ'dʒi:]	Flüchtling
freedom	Freiheit
settler	Siedler/in
immigrant ['ɪmɪɡrənt]	Einwanderer, Einwanderin
persecution [ˌpɜːsɪ'kju:ʃn]	Verfolgung
to persecute ['pɜːsɪkju:t] s.o.	jdn verfolgen
to emigrate	auswandern
famine ['fæmɪn]	Hungersnot
independence	Unabhängigkeit
colonist	Siedler/in (einer Kolonie)
to represent [ˌ– –'–]	vertreten
government	Regierung
tax	Steuer
to resist	Widerstand leisten
to *be at war	Krieg (gegeneinander) führen
Declaration of Independence	Unabhängigkeitserklärung
representative [ˌreprɪ'zentətɪv]	Vertreter/in
document ['– – –]	Dokument, Urkunde
to open up	erschließen
to explore	erforschen
territory	Territorium, Gebiet, Land
to suffer ['sʌfə]	leiden
hardship	schwere Not
to *be on the move	in Bewegung sein, unterwegs sein
frontier	Grenze zwischen Zivilisation u. Wildnis
civilization [ˌsɪvɪlaɪ'zeɪʃn]	Zivilisation, erschlossenes Gebiet

The pioneers travelled west in wagon trains. On their way along the trail, they often had to fight Indians, who were trying to protect their hunting grounds from the white invaders. Some of these native American tribes were fierce and warlike, others were more peaceful. Many treaties were made with the Indians – but were broken again as soon as the whites decided they needed the Indians' land. The Indians' greatest victory – at the Battle of the Little Bighorn in 1876 – was called a massacre by the whites. Fourteen years later, at Wounded Knee, American soldiers killed 300 Sioux men, women and children, although they wished to surrender. Either it was an act of revenge, or a terrible mistake.

Most of the Indians were driven from their land and forced to move to reservations – often thousands of miles from their home. Many Indians died on the way. For those who survived the journey, the new life was hard.

The Indians officially became US citizens in 1928. But they have not forgotten their history, their customs, their heroes, and the ancient traditions of their ancestors.

Slavery in the States

The first black slaves were brought on ships from Africa in the early 17th century. Two hundred years later, the cotton plantations in the Southern states of America depended on slavery. But by the 1830s, slavery had disappeared in the Northern states, where people were firmly against it. The North and South could not come to an agreement, and in 1860 the Southern states left the Union. Abraham Lincoln was President at that time. In order to keep all the states of the Union together, he led the North in the Civil War against the rebellious South. The North won the war in 1865, and slavery in all the States was abolished. Lincoln was assassinated five days after the end of the war.

pioneer [ˌpaɪəˈnɪə]	Pionier/in
wagon [ˈwægən] **train**	Zug von Planwagen
trail	Spur, Weg
to protect	(be)schützen
hunting ground	Jagdgebiet
native [ˈneɪtɪv] *(adj./noun)*	einheimisch; Eingeborene/r
tribe [traɪb]	Stamm
fierce [fɪəs]	wild, grimmig
warlike	kriegerisch
peaceful	friedlich
to ˙make/˙break a treaty	einen Vertrag schließen/brechen
massacre [ˈmæsəkə]	Massaker
to surrender	sich ergeben, kapitulieren
revenge [rɪˈvendʒ]	Rache
to ˙drive s.o. from	*hier:* vertreiben
to force (s.o. to do s.th.)	jdn zwingen, etwas zu tun
reservation [ˌrezəˈveɪʃn]	Reservat
to survive	überleben
citizen [ˈsɪtɪzn]	(Staats-)Bürger/in
custom [ˈkʌstəm]	Sitte
hero, heroine	Held, Heldin
ancient [ˈeɪnʃənt]	uralt
tradition [–ˈ– –]	Tradition
ancestor	Vorfahre/in
slavery [ˈsleɪvərɪ]	Sklaverei
slave [sleɪv]	Sklave, Sklavin
cotton plantation [–ˈ– –]	Baumwollplantage
to ˙come to an agreement	sich einig werden
Union [ˈjuːnjən]	Verband, Union
	(der Vereinigten Staaten)
rebellious	aufständisch, widerstrebend
to abolish [əˈbɒlɪʃ] **s.th.**	etwas abschaffen
to assassinate [əˈsæsɪneɪt] **s.o.**	(aus politischen Gründen) jdn ermorden, ein Attentat auf jdn verüben

3　The Commonwealth: some facts and figures

● The British Commonwealth of Nations came into being in 1926. It consists of 48 states, of many different races and cultures.

● All Commonwealth countries once belonged to the British Empire.

● 100 years ago, the Empire was at its height. It was the biggest empire the world had ever known. Through it, Britain controlled a large part of the world's trade.

● During the 20th century, more and more of Britain's colonies wanted self-government and became independent of the 'mother country'. But by remaining members of the Commonwealth, they kept their link with Britain.

● Many English-sounding place names (Wellington in New Zealand, for example) in Commonwealth countries are reminders of their colonial past.

● The British monarch is Head of the Commonwealth, and also Head of State in some of the countries.

● In the 1950s, a lot of people from the Commonwealth came to work in Britain. Now, about 5% of Britain's population are non-whites and of Commonwealth origin.

to *come into being	entstehen
race	Rasse
culture ['kʌltʃə]	Kultur
empire ['empaɪə]	(Welt-)Reich
100 years ago	vor 100 Jahren
at its height	auf dem Höhepunkt
trade	Handel
self-government	Selbstverwaltung, Unabhängigkeit
independent	unabhängig
member	Mitglied
link	Verbindung, Beziehung
colonial [kə'ləʊnjəl]	kolonial
past	Vergangenheit
Head (of State)	(Staats-)Oberhaupt
non-white	Farbige/r
origin ['ɒrɪdʒɪn]	Herkunft

Girl: *I wish we lived hundreds of years ago!*
Teacher: *Why?*
Girl: *Then there wouldn't be so much history to learn.*

Conflicts

1   Racism and discrimination

Our world is full of conflicts, especially between people of different races, nationalities and cultures. Unfortunately, we all have a natural tendency to feel suspicious of people whose customs or religion, skin colour, language or accent is different from our own. Hatred, aggression and violence towards foreigners or minority groups in the community are often caused by prejudice – that is, by stereotyped ideas about people or things we do not properly understand.

Wherever there is a mixture of races or a clash of cultures, there is racism and discrimination. History is full of examples.

● When slavery came to an end in the USA in 1865, racial prejudice still turned the blacks into second-class citizens. For many years, blacks were still oppressed; they were segregated from whites – in public places like restaurants and buses, and also in American schools. In 1954, when segregation in schools was abolished, there were many whites who reacted against the Supreme Court's decision.

But the struggle for equal rights went on. Martin Luther King, the greatest leader of the Civil Rights Movement, inspired blacks to protest against persecution without using force. He led peaceful demonstrations and protest marches; his aim was tolerance and understanding between black and white.

conflict [ˈkɒnflɪkt]	Konflikt
racism [ˈreɪsɪzm]	Rassismus
discrimination [–,– –ˈ– –]	Diskriminierung
race	Rasse
culture [ˈkʌltʃə]	Kultur
suspicious of s.o./s.th.	misstrauisch gegenüber jdm/etwas
suspicion	Verdacht, Misstrauen
custom [ˈkʌstəm]	Sitte
religion [rɪˈlɪdʒən]	Religion, Glaube
skin colour	Hautfarbe
accent [ˈæksent]	Akzent
hatred [ˈheɪtrɪd]	Hass
aggression [əˈgreʃn]	Aggression, Aggressivität
violence [ˈvaɪələns]	Gewalt, Gewalttätigkeit
violent	gewalttätig
foreigner [ˈfɒrənə]	Ausländer/in
minority [maɪˈnɒrətɪ] **group**	Minderheit
community [kəˈmjuːnətɪ]	Gemeinschaft, Gemeinde
prejudice [ˈpredʒʊdɪs]	Vorurteil, Voreingenommenheit
prejudiced against	voreingenommen gegen
stereotyped [ˈstɪərɪətaɪpt]	klischeehaft, stereotyp
clash	Konflikt, Zusammenstoß,
	Unvereinbarkeit
slavery	Sklaverei
racial prejudice	Rassenvorurteil
second-class citizen [ˈsɪtɪzn]	Bürger/in zweiter Klasse
to oppress [əˈpres]	unterdrücken
to segregate [ˈsegrɪgeɪt]	(nach Rassen) trennen
segregation [ˌsegrɪˈgeɪʃn]	(Rassen-)Trennung
to react against	negativ reagieren auf
struggle	(langer) Kampf
equal rights	gleiche Rechte
Civil [ˈsɪvl] **Rights Movement**	Bürgerrechtsbewegung
to protest [prəˈtest] **(against s.th.)**	(gegen etwas) protestieren
persecution [ˌpɜːsɪˈkjuːʃn]	Verfolgung
to persecute [ˈpɜːsɪkjuːt] s.o.	jdn verfolgen
force	Gewalt
peaceful	friedlich
demonstration [ˌdemənˈstreɪʃn]	Demonstration
protest [ˈprəʊtest] **march**	Protestmarsch
tolerance [ˈtɒlərəns]	Toleranz, Duldsamkeit
understanding	Verständnis

Opportunities for blacks soon improved, but many problems remained. Even today, although African Americans have full equality and are officially integrated, large numbers of them live in ghettos. Successful blacks, who have adapted to the lifestyle of the white community, often feel little sympathy for these poorer ones.

● When the British settled in Australia, the Aboriginals (who had been natives of Australia for 40,000 years) were treated much the same as the Indians in North America. Their way of life was not familiar to the white immigrants, who considered them inferior, drove them off their land and put them into reservations. They did not get equal rights until 1967. Since then, many have assimilated. Some are now discovering their Aboriginal roots. But others feel caught between the two cultures and have no real sense of identity.

● When non-whites from Commonwealth countries began to settle in Britain in growing numbers in the 1960s and 70s, many white people rebelled against the idea of a multi-racial society. Although the Racial Equality Act is now supposed to prevent unfair treatment and discrimination, people's negative attitudes are hard to change.

Intolerance towards ethnic minorities can take many forms. Sometimes people are attacked and beaten up in the streets; others are threatened or damage is done to their homes. Children are sometimes bullied at school or blamed for things they have not done.

Tension between different ethnic groups (between people of African origin, for example, and people from Asia) also causes problems, especially in big cities. People with the same background often live in the same areas, and sometimes form gangs that attack rival groups.

But luckily there are many non-whites in Britain who feel at home in the white community, and at the same time are proud of their own culture. They can enjoy the best of both worlds.

equality [ɪ'kwɒlətɪ] equal	Gleichheit gleich
integrated	eingegliedert, integriert
ghetto	Ghetto
to adapt to s.th.	sich an etwas anpassen
sympathy ['sɪmpəθɪ]	Mitgefühl, Teilnahme
to settle	*hier:* sich niederlassen, sesshaft werden
the Aboriginals [ˌæbə'rɪdʒənəlz]	*die Ureinwohner Australiens*
native ['neɪtɪv]	Eingeborene/r, Ureinwohner/in
to treat	behandeln
way of life	Lebensstil, Lebensart, Lebensweise
familiar [fə'mɪljə]	vertraut, bekannt
immigrant ['ɪmɪgrənt]	Einwanderer, Einwanderin
inferior [ɪn'fɪərɪə]	minderwertig
to *drive s.o. off s.th.	*hier:* jdn von etwas vertreiben
reservation [ˌrezə'veɪʃn]	Reservat
to assimilate [ə'sɪmɪleɪt]	(sich) integrieren, (sich) anpassen
root	Wurzel
to *be caught between two cultures	zwischen zwei Kulturen stehen
sense of identity [aɪ'dentətɪ]	Bewusstsein der eigenen Identität
non-white	Farbige/r
to rebel [rɪ'bel] **(against)**	(gegen etwas) rebellieren
multi-racial society	Gesellschaft, die aus vielen Rassen besteht
Racial Equality Act	Rassengleichheitsgesetz
unfair treatment	ungerechte Behandlung
negative attitude ['ætɪtjuːd]	negative Haltung, Einstellung
intolerance [ɪn'tɒlərəns]	Intoleranz, Unduldsamkeit
ethnic minority [maɪ'nɒrətɪ]	ethnische Minderheit
to attack s.o.	jdn angreifen
to *beat s.o. up	jdn zusammenschlagen
to threaten [θretn] **s.o.**	jdn bedrohen
to *do damage ['dæmɪdʒ] **to s.th.**	etwas beschädigen
to bully ['bʊlɪ] **s.o.**	jdn tyrannisieren
to blame [bleɪm] **s.o.**	jdm die Schuld geben
tension ['tenʃn]	Spannung(en)
ethnic group	ethnische Gruppe
origin ['ɒrɪdʒɪn]	Herkunft
background	Hintergrund: *hier:* Verhältnisse
gang	Bande
rival ['raɪvl] rival *(noun)*	konkurrierend Rivale/-in, Konkurrent/in
to *be proud of s.o./s.th.	auf jdn/etwas stolz sein
the best of both worlds	das Beste aus beiden Welten

• In other European countries there is also conflict between people of different origins. In Germany, guest workers and other foreigners have often been victims of prejudice and unfair treatment. There has been cruelty and hostility towards asylum seekers. Arson attacks on foreigners' homes and on buildings used as temporary homes for refugees have caused tragedy.

Although most people agree that hatred of foreigners is wrong, there have been bitter quarrels in Europe over immigration laws. The influx of so many people applying for political asylum has caused fear and resentment.

2   The troubles of Northern Ireland

This is what some of the people living in Northern Ireland said about the "troubles" of their country before the ceasefire in August 1994.

"I live in a Protestant area of Belfast. I have nothing against Catholics, but I hate the IRA. Another bomb exploded in the city centre last week. Nobody was killed in the explosion this time, but several people were injured. Bomb attacks don't solve problems. These incidents just cause more pain and make the bitterness and hatred worse."

"Northern Ireland should no longer be separated from the Republic of Ireland. I don't like the terrorists' methods, but I believe in what they are fighting for. It isn't right for Protestants to get better jobs and houses than Catholics – just because they are in the majority in this part of Ireland."

"I'm a British soldier. We're here to keep the peace. It's not just the IRA that make trouble. Yesterday two Catholic boys were wounded by gunfire from a van that was driven by a Protestant."

"I'm a police officer with the RUC here in Belfast. Today we arrested two young terrorists who were trying to smuggle a bomb into the city centre. The tragedy is that Catholic and Protestant children mostly grow up separately, so they don't get to know each other."

guest worker	Gastarbeiter/in
victim	Opfer
cruelty cruel [kruəl]	Grausamkeit grausam
hostility [hɒˈstɪlətɪ]	Feindseligkeit
asylum [əˈsaɪləm] **seeker**	Asylsuchende/r, Asylbewerber/in
arson [ˈɑːsn] **attack**	Brandanschlag
refugee [ˌrefjʊˈdʒi]	Flüchtling
tragedy [ˈtrædʒədɪ] tragic	Tragödie tragisch
hatred [ˈheɪtrɪd] **of foreigners** [ˈfɒrənəz]	Fremdenhass, Ausländerfeindlichkeit
bitter	bitter, erbittert
quarrel [ˈkwɒrəl]	Streit, Auseinandersetzung
immigration	Einwanderung
influx [ˈɪnflʌks]	Zustrom
to apply for political asylum [əˈsaɪləm]	um politisches Asyl bitten
fear [fɪə]	Angst, Furcht
resentment [rɪˈzentmənt] to resent	Ärger, Groll übel nehmen
the troubles [ˈtrʌblz] **of N. Ireland**	die Probleme Nordirlands
ceasefire	Einstellung der Kämpfe, Waffenstillstand
Protestant [ˈprɒtɪstənt] *(adj./noun)*	protestantisch, Protestant/in
Catholic [ˈkæθlɪk] *(adj./noun)*	katholisch, Katholik/in
IRA (= Irish Republican Army)	IRA (Irisch-Republikanische Armee)
bomb [bɒm]	Bombe
to explode	explodieren, in die Luft gehen
to kill	töten
explosion [ɪkˈspləʊʒn]	Explosion
to injure [ˈɪndʒə]	verletzen
bomb attack	Bombenangriff, Bombenanschlag
incident [ˈɪnsɪdənt]	Vorfall, Zwischenfall
pain	Schmerz
bitterness	Bitterkeit, Erbittertheit
separated [ˈsepəreɪtɪd] **from**	getrennt von
terrorist [ˈterərɪst] terrorism	Terrorist/in Terrorismus
to *be in the majority [məˈdʒɒrətɪ]	in der Überzahl sein
soldier [ˈsəʊldʒə]	Soldat/in
to *keep the peace	die öffentliche Ordnung wahren
to *make trouble	Schwierigkeiten machen, Unruhe stiften
to wound [wuːnd]	verwunden
gunfire [ˈgʌnˌfaɪə]	*hier:* Schüsse
RUC (= Royal Ulster Constabulary)	*nordirische Polizeibehörde*
to arrest [əˈrest] **s.o.**	jdn verhaften
to smuggle	schmuggeln

3   Crime

Police report alarming rise in organized crime

Britain needs more high security jails

76-year-old woman fined for shoplifting

Student, 21, on trial for rape

Government plans to lock up uncontrollable young offenders

Among 20% of recorded crimes are committed by children under 17. The most common offences are theft and handling stolen goods, and burglary. Other crimes include vandalism and mugging. In extreme cases, children have been found guilty of kidnapping other children, and sometimes even of murder. In 'problem areas' innocent people are often afraid to leave their homes, even in daylight. Many feel that punishments should be more severe. Young offenders cannot be sent to prison. But the Government now plans to allow the courts to put uncontrollable teenage criminals in secure detention centres. These will offer a mixture of vocational training and rehabilitation.

Young man robbed in town centre in broad daylight

After a series of crimes in the Birmingham area, Inspector Smith told newspaper reporters that he is now looking for a man with one eye. If he doesn't find him, he's going to use both eyes.

crime	Verbrechen, Straftat
police *(+ plural verb)*	Polizei
to report	berichten, melden
organized crime	organisiertes Verbrechen
high security jail	Hochsicherheitsgefängnis
jail	Gefängnis
to *go to jail/prison	ins Gefängnis kommen
to fine s.o.	jdn zu einer Geldstrafe verurteilen
fine	Geldstrafe
shoplifting ['–,– –]	Ladendiebstahl
on trial (for) trial	angeklagt (wegen) Prozess
rape	Vergewaltigung
to rob	berauben
robber, robbery	Räuber/in, Raubüberfall
in broad daylight	am helllichten Tag
to lock s.o. up	jdn einsperren
offender	Täter/in, Straffällige/r
to commit a crime	ein Verbrechen begehen
offence [ə'fens]	Straftat, Delikt
theft	Diebstahl
thief (*pl.* thieves)	Dieb/in
handling stolen goods	Hehlerei
to *steal	stehlen
burglary burglar	Einbruch Einbrecher/in
to burgle/to *break into	einbrechen in
vandalism ['– – –]	Vandalismus, Zerstörungswut
vandal, to vandalize	Rowdy, mutwillig zerstören
mugging	Straßenraub
to mug mugger	überfallen Straßenräuber/in
guilty (of)	schuldig
to kidnap kidnapper	entführen Entführer/in
murder	Mord
murderer, to murder	Mörder/in, ermorden
innocent ['– – –]	unschuldig
punishment to punish	Strafe bestrafen
severe [sɪ'vɪə]	hart
prison prisoner	Gefängnis Gefangene/r
court	Gericht
criminal ['krɪmɪnl]	Verbrecher/in
detention centre	Jugendstrafanstalt
vocational training	Berufsausbildung
rehabilitation ['riːə,bɪlɪ'teɪʃn]	Rehabilitation

The media

Every day an enormous stream of information is communicated to the public by 'the media' – that is, by newspapers and magazines, and by television and radio. Most people's ideas and attitudes are influenced greatly by the media – whether they realize it or not!

1 The British press

Nearly everyone in Britain reads newspapers. People buy their papers from a newsagent – or at a newsstand. Some households take more than one daily paper – and two or three different Sunday papers. Most papers are national papers, but there are also local papers with local news. 'Serious' papers include *The Times*, *The Telegraph* and *The Guardian*. Popular papers, which are sometimes called tabloids because of their smaller size, have shorter, more sensational articles, more photos and larger headlines. The best-sellers among them are *The Daily Mail* and *The Daily Express*, *The Mirror* and *The Sun*. The *News of the World* has a very wide circulation; in the early 1990s nearly five million copies were sold each Sunday. The topics that make it so successful are crime, sport and scandal.

As well as the usual columns of newspaper reports, interviews and articles written by journalists, most papers print letters to the editor, crossword puzzles, and advertisements. They often also publish special supplements and colour magazines.

The British have many different weekly and monthly magazines, which cover every interest – from fashion to fishing.

the media ['miːdɪə] *(plural)* medium	die Medien Medium
to communicate	übermitteln, vermitteln
communication	Kommunikation
the public public	die Öffentlichkeit öffentlich
newspaper/paper	Zeitung
magazine [ˌmæɡə'ziːn]	Zeitschrift, Magazin
television	Fernsehen
radio	Radio, Rundfunk
to influence influence	beeinflussen Einfluss
the press	die Presse
newsagent	Zeitungshändler/in
newsstand	Zeitungsstand, -kiosk
daily ['deɪlɪ] **(paper)**	Tageszeitung
Sunday paper	Sonntagszeitung
national paper	überregionale Zeitung
local ['ləʊkl] **paper**	Lokalzeitung
news *(+ singular verb)*	Nachrichten
serious paper	seriöse Zeitung
popular paper	Massenblatt, Boulevardzeitung
tabloid ['tæblɔɪd]	(kleinformatige) Boulevardzeitung
sensational [sen'seɪʃənl]	sensationell
article ['ɑːtɪkl]	Artikel
photo/photograph	Foto, Aufnahme
headline	Schlagzeile
best-seller	Bestseller
circulation [ˌsɜːkjʊ'leɪʃn]	*hier:* Auflage
copy	*hier:* Exemplar
topic	Thema
scandal ['skændəl]	Skandal
column ['kɒləm]	Spalte, Kolumne
report reporter	Bericht Reporter/in
interview ['ɪntəvjuː]	Interview
journalist ['dʒɜːnəlɪst] journalism	Journalist/in Journalismus
to print	drucken
letter to the editor editor	Leserbrief Herausgeber/in
crossword puzzle ['pʌzl]	Kreuzworträtsel
advertisement [əd'vɜːtɪsmənt]	Anzeige, Werbung
to publish publisher	veröffentlichen, herausbringen Verlag
supplement ['sʌplɪmənt]	*hier:* Beilage
colour magazine	Zeitungsbeilage, Magazin
weekly (magazine)	Wochen-(Zeitschrift)
monthly (magazine)	Monats-(Zeitschrift)

2   Television

Some British viewers' opinions:

"Well, I watch TV sometimes – like everyone else. But if there's nothing good on, I switch off. I never sit in front of the set all evening. The programmes I like best are old films, TV plays and serials – the more episodes the better! Sometimes there's a good thriller on a Sunday evening."

"There's a lot of talk about the bad influence of TV – but television isn't just entertainment. It can be very educational. I watch current affairs programmes, like 'Panorama'. And I enjoy documentaries and nature programmes. I find the news is presented best on ITV's 'News at Ten'. But the BBC also have very good newsreaders and announcers."

"We haven't got cable TV in our area, but a few of my friends have got satellite dishes. Trouble is, when there are so many channels to choose from, it's hard to decide what to watch. In my family, we love comedies, cartoons and soap operas, so we all crowd round the telly and turn up the volume when they're on. We also like panel games and variety shows – but not chat shows. Nobody watches breakfast TV in our house – no time!"

"I'm certainly not a TV addict, but I do love watching sport, especially the live outside broadcasts from Wimbledon every summer. The BBC have excellent commentators. If there's one thing I hate, it's TV commercials. Good that there's still no advertising on BBC!"

> – Television will never take the place of newspapers.
> – Why not?
> – Well, have you ever tried killing a fly with a TV set?

viewer	Zuschauer/in
to watch TV	fernsehen
to *be on	(im Fernsehen) laufen
to switch off/on	ausschalten/einschalten
to *sit in front of the (TV) set	vor dem Fernseher sitzen
programme ['prəʊgræm]	Sendung
film *(BE)*	Film
TV play	Fernsehspiel
serial ['sɪərɪəl]	Fernsehserie
episode ['epɪsəʊd]	*hier:* Folge, Fortsetzung
thriller	Thriller, Krimi
entertainment [ˌ– –'– –] to entertain	Unterhaltung unterhalten
educational	*hier:* lehrreich, pädagogisch wertvoll
current affairs	Aktuelles, (politische) Tagesthemen
documentary [ˌdɔkjʊ'mentrɪ]	Dokumentarfilm
to present presenter	*hier:* präsentieren Moderator/in
ITV (= Independent Television)	⎫
the BBC (= British Broadcasting Corporation)	⎬ *britische Fernsehanstalten* ⎭
newsreader	Nachrichtensprecher/in
announcer	Ansager/in, Fernsehsprecher/in
cable ['keɪbl] **TV**	Kabelfernsehen
satellite ['sætəlaɪt] **dish**	Satellitenschüssel
(TV) channel	Kanal, Sender
comedy	Komödie
cartoon	Zeichentrickfilm
soap opera	rührselige Familienserie, Seifenoper
telly *(informal)*	Fernseher, Röhre
to turn up the volume	die Lautstärke aufdrehen
panel ['pænl] **game**	Fernsehquiz (mit Rateteam)
variety [və'raɪətɪ] **show**	Fernsehshow
chat show	Talkshow
breakfast TV	Fernsehen am frühen Morgen, "Frühstücksfernsehen"
to *be a TV addict ['ædɪkt]	vom Fernsehen abhängig sein
live [laɪv]	direkt, live
outside broadcast ['brɔ:dkɑ:st] to *broadcast	nicht im Studio produzierte Sendung senden
commentator	Kommentator/in, Fernsehreporter/in
(TV) commercial [kə'mɜ:ʃl]	Werbespot
advertising ['ædvətaɪzɪŋ]	Werbung

3   Radio

The first radio stations began their transmissions in the 1920s. In Britain, the BBC at first had a national monopoly of the medium. Commercial radio at last became legal in 1972, and by the 1990s almost 100 local radio stations had gone on the air.

Millions of people regularly listen to music on the radio, and there are still many who enjoy listening to radio plays.

4   Cinema

The world's first movie theater was built in Pittsburgh, USA, in 1905. In those days there were only silent films. During and after the First World War, America became dominant in the film industry; Hollywood, with its world-famous studios, was its capital. To produce a film in the classic Hollywood style, actors and actresses, cameramen, producers, writers and technicians all work together, led by a film director.

When television became more and more popular in the 1950s and 1960s, many cinemas had to close. To attract bigger audiences, film-makers began to concentrate more on science fiction and horror films, with fascinating trick photography and other exciting special effects. Big box-office successes were often films containing very violent, ugly scenes. By the 1990s, many people in the USA and in Britain had become worried about the harm done to society by violence on the screen. Film stars were still often idolized. But they were not always the positive role models they had been in the 'golden years' of Hollywood.

A lot of people now watch films at home on video. This means that even the very young may often have access to films that are not suitable for children. Although films and videos are classified, there is no way of checking that parents take the classifications seriously.

A man found a penguin in the park. He took it to a policeman and said, "What should I do with this penguin?"
"Take him to the zoo," said the policeman.
The next day, the policeman saw the same man with the penguin again. "Didn't I tell you to take that penguin to the zoo?" he said.
"I did that yesterday," said the man. "Today I'm taking him to the movies."

radio station	Rundfunkstation, -sender
transmission	Übertragung, Sendung
monopoly [mə'nɒpəlɪ]	Monopol
commercial [kə'mɜ:ʃl] **radio**	Privatsender
local ['ləʊkl] **radio**	Lokalradio, Lokalsender
to *go on the air	gesendet werden, (im Radio) zu hören sein
to listen to (the radio)	(Radio) hören
on the radio	im Radio
radio play	Hörspiel
cinema ['sɪnəmə] *(BE)*	Kino
movie theater *(AE)* movie *(AE)*	Kino Film
silent film	Stummfilm
film industry	Filmindustrie
studio	Studio
to produce (a film)	(einen Film) produzieren
actor, actress	Schauspieler, Schauspielerin
cameraman, camerawoman	Kameramann/-frau
producer	Produzent/in
technician [tek'nɪʃn]	Techniker/in
director	Regisseur/in
to attract	anziehen
attraction [ə'trækʃn]	Attraktion
audience ['ɔ:dɪəns]	Publikum, Zuschauer
filmmaker	Filmhersteller/in, -macher/in
science fiction	Sciencefiction
horror film	Horrorfilm
trick photography [fə'tɒgrəfɪ]	Trickfotografie, Trickaufnahmen
special effects	Spezialeffekte
box-office success [sək'ses]	Kassenschlager
scene [si:n]	Szene
screen	Leinwand, Bildschirm
film star	Filmstar
to idolize ['aɪdəlaɪz]	verehren, vergöttern
idol ['aidl]	Idol
positive role model	Vorbild
video	Video, Filmkassette
to *have access ['ækses] **(to s.th.)**	Zugang (zu etwas) haben
suitable ['su:təbl]	geeignet
to classify	*hier:* nach Gruppen (z.B. 15, 18) einteilen

Politics

1 Parliament and the monarchy in Britain

Britain is not a republic like Germany or the USA. It is a constitutional monarchy. This means that the political power of the King or Queen is limited. He or she has no official right to support or disagree with any particular policy. All political decisions are made by Parliament and the Government.

The British Parliament has two houses: the House of Commons and the House of Lords.

The House of Lords has over a thousand members. Some have inherited their seat, others are made life peers by the monarch. The House of Lords cannot make laws itself; it cannot reject laws that have been passed by the House of Commons. But before a bill can become an Act of Parliament, it must be accepted by the Lords, who can also make their own suggestions.

The House of Commons makes laws, and decides how to spend the taxpayers' money. It is made up of two 'sides': the Members of Parliament belonging to the party in power, and those belonging to the Opposition.

General elections

There are over 650 constituencies in Britain. In a general election, the voters elect one candidate in each of these constituencies. This is decided by majority vote: the person that most people in a constituency have voted for becomes a Member of Parliament. The party with the most MPs has the right to form a government, and the party leader becomes Prime Minister. He or she chooses the ministers to be in charge of different government departments. The party or parties that have lost the election now form the Opposition.

politics ['pɒlɪtɪks] political	Politik politisch
Parliament ['pɑːləmənt]	Parlament
monarchy ['mɒnəkɪ]	Monarchie
republic [rɪ'pʌblɪk]	Republik
constitutional [ˌkɒnstɪ'tjuːʃənl]	verfassungsmäßig, konstitutionell
power in power	Macht an der Macht
to *be limited	begrenzt sein
official	offiziell
right	Recht
to support	unterstützen
to disagree with s.o./s.th.	nicht einverstanden sein mit jdm/etwas
policy	eine Politik, 'Linie'
decision [dɪ'sɪʒn] to decide	Entscheidung (sich) entscheiden
government	Regierung
the House of Commons	das Unterhaus
the House of Lords	das Oberhaus
to inherit [ɪn'herɪt]	erben, vererben
seat	Sitz
life peer [pɪə]	Mitglied des Oberhauses auf Lebenszeit
to *make a law	ein Gesetz entwerfen
to reject [rɪ'dʒekt] **a law**	ein Gesetz verwerfen
to pass a law	ein Gesetz verabschieden
bill	Gesetzesvorlage
Act of Parliament	vom Parlament verabschiedetes Gesetz
to accept	annehmen, akzeptieren
taxpayer	Steuerzahler/in
Member of Parliament (MP)	Parlamentsabgeordnete/r
(political) party	Partei
the Opposition [ˌɒpə'zɪʃn]	die Opposition
general election [ɪ'lekʃn]	Parlamentswahlen
constituency [kən'stɪtjʊənsɪ]	Wahlkreis
voter vote	Wähler/in Stimme
to elect [ɪ'lekt]	wählen
candidate ['kændɪdət]	Kandidat/in
majority [mə'dʒɒrətɪ] **vote**	Mehrheitswahl
to vote for/against s.o.	für/gegen jdn stimmen
to form a government	eine Regierung bilden
leader	*hier:* Vorsitzende/r
prime [praɪm] **minister**	Premierminister/in
minister	Minister/in
to *be in charge of s.th.	verantwortlich sein für etwas
government department	Ministerium

Political parties

For many years, the two leading parties in Britain have been the Conservative Party and the Labour Party. Because of the voting system, smaller parties, such as the Liberal Democrats, have never come to power. They would naturally welcome a change to proportional representation, the system used in Germany, as it might give them the chance to form part of a coalition. But the two-party system is one of Britain's firmest traditions.

Does Britain still need the monarchy? – Two opinions

I am a taxpayer. And I don't see why the state should use my taxes in order to pay for the privileges of people who happen to be princes and princesses, dukes and duchesses.

In a democracy, all representatives of the people should be elected. But in this country, a small group of titled people are allowed to enjoy a life of luxury which the rest of us have to pay for. And what thanks do we get? Every day the papers are full of the latest scandal about the Royal Family.

It is time for the public to say 'no' to all this. The monarchy has no place in a modern society. It stands in the way of equality and progress.

Y. Keeper-King, Oxford

The monarchy is the one political institution that everyone can identify with. All true patriots want to keep the monarchy. The Royal Family have many duties, and they serve our nation well.

Politicians are often corrupt, but the Royal Family are above party politics. They stand for all that is best in this country.

Officially, we are ruled by our monarch. If we abolished the monarchy, who would represent the country as its Head of State? Who would do the Royal Family's work for charities and other important organizations? Now we are 'subjects'; then we would be 'citizens'. And all our colourful ceremonies – like the state opening of Parliament – would disappear for ever. How sad!

Roy L. Fan, Manchester

Conservative (Tory) Party	
Labour ['leɪbə] **Party**	*politische Parteien in GB*
Liberal ['lɪbərəl] **Democrats**	
voting system	Wahlsystem
to *come to power	an die Macht kommen
proportional representation	Verhältniswahl
coalition [ˌkəʊə'lɪʃn]	Koalition
two-party system	Zweiparteiensystem
tradition [trə'dɪʃn]	Tradition
state	Staat
tax	Steuer
privilege ['prɪvɪlɪdʒ]	Sonderrecht, Privileg
prince princess	Prinz Prinzessin
duke [djuːk] **duchess** ['dʌtʃɪs]	Herzog Herzogin
democracy [dɪ'mɒkrəsɪ]	Demokratie
representative	Vertreter/in
the people *(singular)*	das Volk
titled ['taɪtld] title ['taɪtl]	mit Adelstitel Titel
scandal ['skændl]	Skandal
the Royal Family	die Königliche Familie
the public public	die Öffentlichkeit öffentlich
society [sə'saɪətɪ]	Gesellschaft
equality [iː'kwɒlətɪ] equal	Gleichheit gleich
progress *(singular only)*	Fortschritt(e)
institution [ˌɪnstɪ'tjuːʃn]	Einrichtung, Institution
to identify [aɪ'dentɪfaɪ] **with s.o./s.th.**	sich mit jdm/etwas identifizieren
patriot ['pætrɪət] patriotic	Patriot/in patriotisch
duty ['djuːtɪ] to do one's duty	Pflicht, Aufgabe seine Pflicht tun
to serve	dienen
politician [ˌpɒlɪ'tɪʃn]	Politiker/in
corrupt [kə'rʌpt]	bestechlich, korrupt
party politics	Parteipolitik
to rule	herrschen über, regieren
monarch ['mɒnək]	Monarch/in
to abolish [ə'bɒlɪʃ] **s.th.**	etwas abschaffen
Head of State	Staatsoberhaupt
charity ['tʃærətɪ]	Wohltätigkeitsverein
subject ['sʌbdʒɪkt]	*hier:* Untertan/in
citizen ['sɪtɪzn]	(Staats-)Bürger/in
ceremony ['serɪmənɪ]	Zeremonie, Feierlichkeit

2   The American political system

The American Government has three branches: the President, Congress and the Supreme Court.

The President

The President of the USA is the Head of State, and is elected by the people. Before this, he or she has to be nominated by delegates of his or her party. The President stays in office for four years, and may be re-elected for one more term of four years.

A presidential election is a major event in the USA. The candidates who run for office have a very busy time – making speeches and leading the election campaign.

The President is the political leader of the country and is also its chief representative. In this way the President combines the functions of the monarch and the Prime Minister in Britain. This makes the American President a very influential figure. The President's family, known as the 'First Family', are also very much in the public eye.

Congress

While the President represents the executive branch (the Administration), Congress is the legislative branch of the American government: its job is to make laws.

Congress consists of two houses: the House of Representatives and the Senate. Each of the 50 American states has two senators in the Senate, however big or small the state is. The number of representatives in the House of Representatives depends on the population of each state.

branch [brɑ:ntʃ]	Zweig
president ['– – –]	Präsident/in
Congress ['kɒŋgres]	Kongress, *das amerikanische Parlament*
the Supreme [sʊ'pri:m] **Court**	*der Oberste Gerichtshof der USA*
to nominate	ernennen
delegate	bevollmächtigte/r Vertreter/in, Delegierte/r
in office	im Amt
to re-elect s.o.	jdn wiederwählen
term	*hier:* Amtszeit
event [–'–]	Ereignis
to *run for office	für ein Amt kandidieren
to *make a speech	eine Rede halten
election campaign [kæm'peɪn]	Wahlkampf, Wahlkampagne
function ['fʌŋkʃn]	Aufgabe, Funktion
influential [ˌɪnflʊ'enʃl]	einflussreich
the First Family	Präsidentenfamilie (USA)
in the public eye	im Blickpunkt der Öffentlichkeit
executive [ɪg'zekjʊtɪv] **branch**	Exekutive
Administration (*BE* Government)	*hier:* Regierung
legislative ['ledʒɪslətɪv] **branch**	Legislative
the House of Representatives	das Repräsentantenhaus
the Senate ['senɪt]	der Senat, *Teil des amerikanischen Parlaments*
state	(Bundes-)Staat
senator ['senətə]	Senator/in
population [ˌpɒpjʊ'leɪʃn]	*hier:* Einwohnerzahl

The Supreme Court

The Supreme Court is the highest court in the USA. It watches over the American Constitution, and decides if a law or a decision of a lower court is unconstitutional.

The system of checks and balances

While the British Prime Minister (like the German Chancellor) is the leader of the government and also a Member of Parliament, the three branches in America are clearly separated. A British prime minister could not govern if his or her party didn't have the majority in Parliament. But American presidents have often been faced with a majority of the other party in Congress. The two major parties are the Democrats and the Republicans.

How the branches check on each other:

- The President can veto laws passed by Congress.
  But Congress can overrule the President's veto if there is a two-thirds majority in favour of the law.

- The President appoints judges to the Supreme Court.
  But the Court has the power to decide whether Presidential Acts are constitutional or not.

- The Senate must confirm the judges chosen by the president for the Supreme Court.
  On the other hand, the Supreme Court can declare laws passed by Congress as unconstitutional.

Washington is the seat of the American Federal Government. Each state also has a separate constitution, a state senate, and its own governor and courts of justice.

unconstitutional	verfassungswidrig
system of checks and balances	System der Gewaltenteilung und gegenseitigen Gewaltenkontrolle
chancellor ['tʃɑ:nsələ]	Kanzler/in
to separate ['sepəreɪt]	trennen
separate ['seprət]	getrennt
to govern	regieren
to *have the majority [mə'dʒɒrətɪ]	die Mehrheit haben
the Democrats ['deməkræts]	*die zwei wichtigsten*
the Republicans [rɪ'pʌblɪkənz]	*Parteien der USA*
to veto ['vi:təʊ]	Veto einlegen gegen
to overrule	ablehnen, überstimmen
to *be in favour of s.th.	für etwas sein
to appoint [ə'pɔɪnt] **s.o.**	jdn ernennen
judge [dʒʌdʒ]	Richter/in
to judge	richten, urteilen über
to confirm	bestätigen
to declare	*hier:* erklären
federal	Bundes-
governor ['gʌvənə]	Gouverneur/in
court of justice	Gerichtshof
justice ['dʒʌstɪs]	Gerechtigkeit

"In the name of democracy, welcome! Up to now we've had a one-party system."

3   Europe – and European Union

The origins of the European Community (EC) date back to the 1950s, when the idea of economic cooperation between European countries was first developed. At first, the Common Market, as it was then often called, had six member states. Britain did not join until 1973. At the beginning of the 1990s, a plan for full economic union, with a European bank, fixed exchange rates, and eventually a single currency, the ecu, was agreed on.

Here are some opinions:

All in all, I'm in favour of free trade within Europe, but I'm against political union. There are so many different countries in Europe. You can't expect them all to want the same policies just because they're linked together by the EU!

Mobility for students and teachers is one of the main advantages of a united Europe. In the past, British qualifications, diplomas and so on, were often not recognized in other European countries – and vice versa. Now there'll be better opportunities for people who want to move around.

It's a good thing for Europe to be united, especially in foreign policy. But I'm afraid there'll be a lot of unnecessary regulations and bureaucracy!

I think it's so important to break down the barriers between European countries. Going abroad is much pleasanter now that customs and passport control at borders have been relaxed.

I don't like the idea of the ecu. Regional diversity and individuality are vital to people's feelings of identity and national pride. These days everything is 'Euro' – from Euro toilet seats to the Eurotunnel!

the European Union ['juːnjən] **(EU)**	die Europäische Union (EU)
origin ['ɒrɪdʒɪn]	Ursprung, Herkunft
European Community (EC)	die Europäische Gemeinschaft (EG)
economic cooperation [kəʊˌɒpəˈreɪʃn]	wirtschaftliche Zusammenarbeit
the Common Market	der Gemeinsame Markt
member state	Mitgliedsland
to join	beitreten
economic union ['juːnjən]	wirtschaftliche Union
bank	Bank, Geldinstitut
exchange rate [reɪt]	Wechselkurs
eventually [ɪˈventʃʊəlɪ]	schließlich, nach einer gewissen Zeit
single currency ['kʌrənsɪ]	einheitliche Währung
ecu	Ecu
free trade	Freihandel
political union ['juːnjən]	politische Vereinigung, Union
to link	verbinden, aneinander koppeln
mobility mobile ['məʊbaɪl]	Beweglichkeit, Mobilität mobil
advantage disadvantage	Vorteil Nachteil
united	vereinigt
qualifications	*hier:* Zeugnisse
diploma	Diplom
to recognize	*hier:* anerkennen
vice versa [ˌvaɪsɪˈvɜːsə]	umgekehrt
opportunity [ˌɒpəˈtjuːnətɪ]	Gelegenheit, Chance
foreign ['fɒrən] **policy**	Außenpolitik
regulation	Vorschrift, Regelung
bureaucracy [bjʊəˈrɒkrəsɪ]	Bürokratie
to *break down	abbauen
barrier ['bærɪə]	Mauer, Barriere
customs *(plural only)*	Zoll
passport control	Passkontrolle
border	Grenze
to relax	*hier:* lockern
diversity [daɪˈvɜːsətɪ]	Vielfalt
individuality ['ɪndɪˌvɪdʒʊˈælətɪ]	Individualität
to *be vital ['vaitl] **to**	lebenswichtig sein für
identity [aɪˈdentətɪ]	Identität
national pride	Nationalstolz
Euro ['jʊərəʊ]	Europa-orientiert, 'Euro-'
Eurotunnel ['jʊərəʊtʌnl]	Tunnel unter dem Ärmelkanal
(= Channel Tunnel)	

World problems

1   Growth

The biggest problem that the world faces today is the problem of growth.

● World population is growing faster and faster, and more and more people are starving. If the present rate of growth continues, the population of the earth will have doubled in only 40 years.

● Industrial production is also growing. This has led to a rise in the material standard of living – but it has also resulted in pollution of the environment.

● Pollution is growing, too. The earth's atmosphere, for example, contains more and more carbon dioxide as the years go by. This is mainly because of the burning of fossil fuels and the destruction of forests.

● Cities are growing, the use of fertilizers is growing; nuclear wastes (the by-products of nuclear power production) and other waste products are building up; traffic is increasing, more and more energy is being consumed, and more and more natural resources are being used up.

world	Welt
growth to *grow	Wachstum wachsen
population	Bevölkerung
to starve	(ver)hungern
rate [reɪt]	Rate
earth	Erde
to double ['dʌbl]	(sich) verdoppeln
industrial [ɪn'dʌstrɪəl] **production**	industrielle Produktion
industry	Industrie
rise to *rise	Anstieg steigen
material [mə'tɪərɪəl] *(adj.)*	materiell
material	Stoff
standard of living	Lebensstandard
to result in result	führen zu Folge, Ergebnis
pollution	(Umwelt-)Verschmutzung
to pollute	verschmutzen
environment	Umwelt
atmosphere ['– –,–]	Atmosphäre
carbon dioxide ['kɑːbəndaɪ'ɒksaɪd]	Kohlendioxyd
to *burn	(ver)brennen
fossil ['fɒsl] **fuel**	fossiler Brennstoff
destruction to destroy	Zerstörung zerstören
forest	Wald
fertilizer	Dünger, Düngemittel
nuclear ['njuːklɪə]	Kern-, Atom-, nuklear
waste	*hier:* Müll, Abfall, Nebenprodukt
by-product ['baɪ,prɒdʌkt]	Nebenprodukt
nuclear ['njuːklɪə] **power**	Atomkraft, Kernenergie
waste product	Abfallstoff, Abfallprodukt
to *build up	*hier:* (sich) ansammeln
traffic	Verkehr
to increase [–'–]	zunehmen, stärker werden
increase ['– –]	Zunahme, Steigerung
energy ['enədʒɪ]	Energie
to consume [kən'sjuːm]	verbrauchen
consumer	Verbraucher/in
natural resources [rɪ'sɔːsɪz]	Bodenschätze, Naturschätze
to use s.th. up	etwas aufbrauchen

2   The results of growth

Traditionally, the idea of growth has been welcomed. In rich countries, economic growth is mostly seen – at least by politicians – as a sign of progress. In poor parts of the world, a large family promises parents economic security and hope for the future.

But there are limits to the earth's capacity for growth. For example, in order to survive, a growing population needs larger and larger supplies of fresh water, food, raw materials and fossil fuels. At the same time, the earth has to absorb more and more waste and pollution. Unfortunately, the sources of materials and energy cannot last forever – and the earth cannot go on absorbing all our waste products without showing signs of damage. The 'holes' in the ozone layer are one example of the damage that is being done. Another is the 'greenhouse effect', which is likely to cause a global climate change, with long-term effects that are very difficult to predict.

It seems certain that if growth is allowed to continue, the situation on our planet will get out of control: eventually there will be food shortages, energy and materials that cannot be replaced will run out; because of pollution and shortages, diseases will spread more easily, and there will be a dramatic decline in our health.

3   Did you know?

The number of cars on the roads has doubled in less than 20 years. But worldwide, fewer than one in ten people own a car. Hundreds of millions of people live in poor housing – or are homeless – and have no chance of owning washing-machines, televisions or cars anyway.

Exhaust fumes are already helping to cause acid rain and to harm the ecology. So what will happen when the standard of living in Third World countries improves – and everyone everywhere wants a car?

B. Green, York

economic growth	Wirtschaftswachstum
progress *(singular only)*	Fortschritt(e)
security secure	Sicherheit sicher
future	Zukunft
limit to limit	Grenze begrenzen
capacity [kə'pæsətɪ]	Kapazität, Belastbarkeit
to survive	überleben
supply [sə'plaɪ]	Vorrat, Versorgung
to supply with	versorgen mit
raw materials	Rohstoffe
to absorb [əb'zɔːb] s.th.	etwas aufnehmen, aufsaugen
source [sɔːs]	Quelle
to last	*hier:* reichen, ausreichen, halten
long-lasting	dauerhaft
damage ['dæmɪdʒ] to damage	Schaden schaden, beschädigen, verderben
ozone ['əʊzəʊn] **layer**	Ozonschicht
greenhouse effect	Treibhauseffekt
to cause s.th.	etwas verursachen
global ['gləʊbl] globe	global, weltweit Erdkugel
climate ['klaɪmɪt] **change**	Klimaveränderung
long-term effect	Langzeitwirkung
to predict prediction	voraussagen, vorhersagen Voraussage
planet ['plænɪt]	Planet
to *get out of control	außer Kontrolle geraten
eventually [ɪ'ventʃʊəlɪ]	schließlich, nach einer gewissen Zeit
shortage ['ʃɔːtɪdʒ]	Knappheit, Mangel
to replace [rɪ'pleɪs]	ersetzen
to *run out	*hier:* ausgehen, zu Ende gehen
disease [dɪ'ziːz]	Krankheit
to *spread [spred]	(sich) ausbreiten
decline [dɪ'klaɪn]	Rückgang, Verschlechterung
to decline	zurückgehen, sich verschlechtern
health healthy	Gesundheit gesund
worldwide *(adj. & adv.)* ['–'–]	weltweit
housing ['haʊzɪŋ]	Unterkunft, Wohnung
homeless	obdachlos, heimatlos
exhaust [ɪg'zɔːst] **fumes**	Abgase
acid rain [,æsɪd'reɪn]	saurer Regen
to harm s.th./s.o.	etwas/jdm Schaden zufügen, etwas schädigen, jdn verletzen
ecology [iː'kɒlədʒɪ]	Ökologie
ecological [,iːkə'lɒdʒɪkl]	ökologisch
Third World	Dritte Welt

4   What can be done?

Here are some of the things you can do to help save our planet:

● Use your car as little as you can, and share it whenever possible. You can also increase fuel efficiency by driving more slowly.

● Always sort your rubbish before you throw it away: Buy drinks in returnable bottles whenever you can. But if there is no deposit on your bottles, don't just throw them in the dustbin. Take them to a bottle bank. Your local recycling centre also has 'banks' for old cans and newspapers. Re-use paper, plastic bags, etc., as much as you can.

● Buy local food (to cut down the pollution caused by transporting food around the world), and eat less meat (so more land is free for forests – and for wildlife).

● Support plans for alternative technology (e.g. the use of solar energy to heatwater; waterpower or windpower to generate electricity).

● Develop your own environment-friendly lifestyle. (Choose hobbies – or holidays – that are energy-saving and do not require too much equipment, for example.)

● Support an organization that helps people in Third World countries (e.g. improving education and birth control, helping to fight against poverty and famine). Every donation is useful.

● Don't be pessimistic or cynical about the world's problems. Be optimistic, and be willing to try out new ideas.

Act now!
Make an effort before WE become
the world's next endangered species!

"We made it! We made it! We're on the Endangered Species list!"

to save	*hier:* retten
to share	(mit anderen) teilen
efficiency [ɪ'fɪʃənsɪ] efficient	Leistungsfähigkeit leistungsfähig
to sort (one's) rubbish	(seinen) Müll sortieren
to *throw s. th. away	etwas wegwerfen
returnable bottle	Pfandflasche
deposit [dɪ'pɒzɪt]	Pfand
dustbin	Mülleimer, Mülltonne
bottle bank	Altglascontainer
recycling	Wiederverwertung, Recycling
to recycle	wieder verwerten
to re-use	wieder verwenden
plastic bag	Plastiktüte
to *cut down	reduzieren
to transport [–'–]	transportieren
transport ['– –]	Transport
wildlife ['waɪldˌlaɪf]	Tierwelt (Tiere in freier Wildbahn)
to support support	unterstützen Unterstützung
alternative technology [–'– – – –]	alternative Technologie
solar ['səʊlə] **energy**	Sonnenenergie
waterpower	Wasserkraft
windpower	Windenergie
to generate	erzeugen
electricity electric	Strom elektrisch
environment(ally)-friendly	umweltfreundlich
lifestyle	Lebensstil
energy-saving	energiesparend
equipment [ɪ'kwɪpmənt]	Ausrüstung
to equip	ausrüsten
birth control	Geburtenkontrolle
poverty ['pɒvətɪ] poor	Armut arm
famine ['fæmɪn]	Hungersnot
donation [dəʊ'neɪʃn] to donate	Spende spenden
pessimistic [ˌ– –'– –]	pessimistisch
pessimist ['– – –]	Pessimist/in
cynical ['sɪnɪkl]	zynisch
optimistic [ˌ– –'– –]	optimistisch
optimist ['– – –]	Optimist/in
to try s. th. out	etwas ausprobieren
to *make an effort ['efət]	sich anstrengen, sich bemühen
endangered species ['spiːʃiːz]	(vom Aussterben) bedrohte Art
to endanger	gefährden

Education

1   The school system in Britain

a)   State schools

In Britain, children first go to school when they are five. They usually go to primary school until they are eleven. After that they go to secondary school. There are a few state grammar schools, but most pupils attend comprehensive schools. The first-year classes at these schools are of mixed ability, but after that they are usually divided into different groups for lessons in academic subjects.

b)   Independent schools

Independent schools are not run by the state; they are fee-paying private schools. Many of them are boarding schools. Among them are the famous public schools, such as Eton, Harrow and Rugby, which have very old traditions and usually have a high academic standard. Many of these private schools are boys' or girls' schools, but some are co-educational (mixed schools).

c)   School work and examinations

Most schools set exams twice a year, to test pupils' ability. School reports come out at the end of each term, or at least twice a year. At the age of 15 or 16, pupils take their GCSEs (General Certificate of Secondary Education); GCSE results depend on course work as well as written examinations.

Up to GCSE, English, one foreign language and Maths are compulsory subjects on the curriculum, but pupils take courses that are appropriate to their ability.

education [ˌedʒʊˈkeɪʃn]	Erziehung, Ausbildung
to educate	erziehen, ausbilden
state school	staatliche Schule
to *go to school	in die Schule gehen
primary [ˈpraɪmərɪ] **school**	Grundschule
secondary [ˈsekəndrɪ] **school**	weiter führende Schule
grammar school	*etwa:* Gymnasium
pupil [ˈpjuːpl]	Schüler/in
to attend (a school)	(eine Schule) besuchen
comprehensive [ˌkɒmprɪˈhensɪv] **school**	Gesamtschule
(mixed) ability	(unterschiedliche) Begabung, Fähigkeit
lesson	(Unterrichts)stunde
academic subject	naturwissenschaftliches u. geistes-wissenschaftliches Schulfach
independent school	(vom Staat) unabhängige Schule, Privatschule
to *be run by the state	staatlich geführt werden
to *pay a fee [fiː]	*hier:* Schulgeld bezahlen
private school	Privatschule
boarding school	Internat
public [ˈpʌblɪk] **school**	Privatschule (von hohem Rang)
academic standard	schulisches Niveau
co-educational (school)	(Schule) für Mädchen und Jungen
mixed school	gemischte Schule
examination	Prüfung, Examen
to *set an exam	*hier:* eine Prüfung abhalten
to test test	überprüfen, kontrollieren Test
(school) report	Zeugnis
term	Trimester *(in GB wird das Schuljahr in drei Trimester geteilt)*
to *take an exam	eine Prüfung schreiben, machen
General Certificate [səˈtɪfɪkət] **of Secondary Education (GCSE)**	*Prüfung, die etwa Realschul-/Hauptschulabschluss entspricht*
result [rɪˈzʌlt]	Ergebnis
course work	schriftliche Leistung innerhalb eines Schuljahres
written exam(ination)	schriftliche Prüfung
foreign language	Fremdsprache
Maths [mæθs] **(= Mathematics)**	Mathe
compulsory [kəmˈpʌlsərɪ]	obligatorisch, Pflicht-
curriculum [kəˈrɪkjələm]	Lehrplan
appropriate (to)	angemessen, geeignet (für)

Optional subjects on the timetable include Art, Biology, Business Studies, Chemistry, Computer Studies, Craft Design and Technology, Geography and History, Information Technology, Modern Languages, Music, Physical Education, Physics, Religious Studies, and Social Studies.

After GCSE, most people leave school and go to a technical college, do two years training on YTS, or look for a job without a training course.

But it is possible to stay on at school for two more years, in the sixth form, to prepare for A-Level exams. This can also be done at sixth form college. If you want to go to university you usually need good marks in at least two A-Level subjects as qualifications. A-Levels include practical exams (in science subjects, for example) and oral exams (in languages). If you do not pass a subject at A-Level, you can re-sit the exams in the subject you failed. It is usual to choose A-Level subjects which will be useful in your later career. For example, if you want to study French and German at university, good exam results in these subjects will be expected when you apply for a place.

First student: *How were your exam questions?*
Second student: *They were easy! But I had trouble with the answers.*

optional	fakultativ, Wahl-
timetable	*hier:* Stundenplan
Art	Kunst
Biology [baɪˈɒlədʒɪ]	Biologie
Business [ˈbɪznɪs] **Studies**	Wirtschaftskunde
Chemistry [ˈkemɪstrɪ]	Chemie
Computer Studies	EDV
Craft [krɑːft] **Design & Technology** [tekˈnɒlədʒɪ]	*etwa:* Handarbeits- und Werksunterricht
Geography [dʒɪˈɒgrəfɪ]	Erdkunde
History	Geschichte
Information Technology	Informatik
Modern Languages	moderne Fremdsprachen
Music [ˈmjuːzɪk]	Musik
Physical Education (PE)	Sport (als Schulfach)
Physics [ˈfɪzɪks]	Physik
Religious [rɪˈlɪdʒəs] **Studies**	Religion (als Schulfach)
Social Studies	Gesellschaftskunde
to *leave school	die Schule verlassen, von der S. abgehen
technical college	technische Fachschule
training to train	Ausbildung, Lehre ausbilden
YTS [ˈwaɪtiːˈes] **(= Youth Training Scheme)**	berufliches Ausbildungsprogramm
training course	Lehre, Berufsausbildung
sixth form	Oberstufe (die letzten 2 Schuljahre)
A-Level (= Advanced Level)	*etwa:* Abitur
sixth form college	Schule, die Oberstufenschüler auf 'A-Level' vorbereitet
to *go to university	studieren
mark	(Schul-)Note
qualification [ˌkwɒlɪfɪˈkeɪʃn]	Qualifikation, Voraussetzung
practical exam	praktische Prüfung
oral [ˈɔːrəl] **exam**	mündliche Prüfung
to pass (an exam)	(eine Prüfung) bestehen
to *sit/re-sit (an exam)	(eine Prüfung) machen/wiederholen
to fail (an exam)	(in einer Prüfung) durchfallen
to *choose choice	wählen Wahl
career [kəˈrɪə]	Laufbahn, Beruf, Karriere
to study (French)	(Französisch) studieren
to apply for a place	sich um einen (Studien-)Platz bewerben

On the school notice-board

> Friday, 4.45 p.m.:
> Choir practice (with orchestra!)
> in the Assembly Hall.

> Who left their PE kit (new!)
> on the sports ground after
> Games last Wednesday?
> Please collect from the
> staffroom!

> Why not join the Photo Club?
> Meetings: In the new library
> during the lunch break on
> Tuesdays.

Rules

● No smoking in school or in the school grounds.

● Leave your bicycles only in the bicycle shed behind the playground.

● Food may only be eaten in the cafeteria, never in the classrooms or corridors.

● The science laboratories, the language lab and the gym are out of bounds except when a member of staff is present.

● Remember to bring a doctor's certificate if you are absent for more than 5 days.

– The Headmaster –

2   School in the USA

Different words for the same thing ...

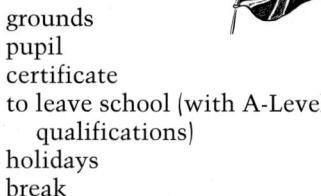

in American English	in British English
elementary school	primary school
high school	secondary school
grade	class
campus	grounds
student	pupil
diploma	certificate
to graduate (from high school)	to leave school (with A-Level qualifications)
vacation	holidays
recess	break
principal	head(teacher)
janitor	caretaker
public school	state school

notice-board	Schwarzes Brett, Anschlagbrett
choir ['kwaɪə] **practice**	Chorprobe
orchestra ['ɔːkɪstrə]	Orchester
assembly hall	Aula
kit	Ausrüstung, 'Zeug'
sports ground	Sportplatz
Games	(Mannschafts-)Spiele (als Schulfach)
staffroom	Lehrerzimmer
staff [stɑːf]	Lehrpersonal
to join a club	*hier:* in eine AG eintreten
meeting	Treffen, Versammlung
library ['laɪbrərɪ]	Bibliothek
lunch break	Mittagspause
rule	Regel, Vorschrift
school rules	Schulordnung
grounds *(plural only)*	Gelände
bicycle shed	Fahrradschuppen, Fahrradunterstand
playground	Schulhof
cafeteria [ˌkæfɪ'tɪərɪə]	Cafeteria
classroom	Klassenzimmer
corridor ['kɒrɪdɔː]	Gang
science laboratory [lə'bɒrətrɪ]	Labor (für Naturwissenschaften)
language lab(oratory) [læb]	Sprachlabor
gym [dʒɪm] (= **gym**nasium)	Turnhalle
[dʒɪm'neɪzjəm]	
out of bounds	nicht zu betreten
member of staff	Lehrkraft
to *be present	anwesend sein
doctor's certificate [sə'tɪfɪkət]	ärztliches Attest
to *be absent ['æbsənt]	fehlen, abwesend sein
headmaster headmistress	Schuldirektor Schuldirektorin
(also: **head, headteacher**)	
janitor ['dʒænɪtə] *(AE)*, **caretaker** *(BE)*	Hausmeister/in

Mum: *Come on, John! You'll be late for school.*
John: *I don't want to go to school. The teachers don't like me, the children don't like me. Nobody likes me.*
Mum: *But you have to go, John.*
John: *Why should I?*
Mum: *You know quite well! Firstly, you're 46 years old, and secondly, you're the headmaster.*

3   School in Germany

Nick Burton spent six months at a school in Germany. When he got back home, he told his friends about the system in Germany...

"It's hard to explain in English about school life in Germany. This is because a lot of German traditions and institutions have no real equivalent in Britain.

There wasn't a comprehensive school where I stayed, but three different types of school. I went to a 'Realschule' – that's a secondary school where pupils leave at 16. There was no school uniform! Instead of revising for school exams every summer like we do, German pupils work for class tests all through the year. So you can't be lazy for long! Marks in these tests seemed very important, especially near the end of the school year, when most people worked out their average marks even before the reports came out! In Germany the best mark is 1 (like Grade A with us), and the worst is 6 (that's a fail). Some parents pay for their children to have private coaching in subjects they are bad at. In my class, two people stayed down because of bad marks.

Schools in Germany have rules of course, like we do, and you are punished if you break them. If you behave badly or don't hand work in, you may be kept in after school, or you may be given extra work. If you cheat in tests – or copy from your neighbour – some teachers won't mark your paper, but will give you a 6 automatically! Sometimes a person's name is put down in the register – that's a bit like an order mark. If you get too many order marks, you may be suspended, or even expelled!

One afternoon it was very hot and my friend and I skipped PE and went swimming instead. Sometimes lessons are cancelled when the weather is really hot. In the summer most classes go on an excursion, and sometimes there's a day out too. It rained non-stop on our day out!

People at the school I was at get a school leaving certificate at the end of the 10th year. It's a bit like our GCSEs, but you don't have to do written exams in all parts of Germany. I had another friend who was at the grammar school (she was a form captain). They take their school leaving exams three years later. These are like A-Levels, except that you have to take courses in more subjects – they can't drop as many as we can. They usually do two main subjects, and several other subjects."

Pupil:	*Should someone be punished for something they haven't done?*
Teacher:	*No, of course not!*
Pupil:	*Good – I haven't done my homework.*

equivalent [ɪˈkwɪvələnt]	Entsprechung
school uniform [ˈjuːnɪfɔːm]	Schuluniform
to revise [rɪˈvaɪz] (for an exam)	sich durch Wiederholen des Stoffes (auf eine Prüfung) vorbereiten
revision [rɪˈvɪʒn]	Wiederholung
to work (for a test)	lernen (für eine Arbeit)
class test	Klassenarbeit
lazy	faul
to work out	ausrechnen
average	Durchschnitt
Grade A	Note 1
fail [feɪl]	Note 6 (durchgefallen)
private coaching [ˈkəʊtʃɪŋ]	Nachhilfe
to *be bad (good/brilliant) at (a subject)	schlecht (gut/hervorragend) sein in (einem Fach)
to stay down	sitzen bleiben
to punish s.o. punishment	jdn bestrafen Strafe
to behave [bɪˈheɪv] (well/badly)	sich (gut/schlecht) verhalten
behaviour [bɪˈheɪvjə]	Verhalten
to hand work in	Arbeit, Hausaufgaben abgeben
to *be kept in	nachsitzen
extra work	eine Strafarbeit
to cheat	schummeln, mogeln
to copy	abschreiben
to mark a paper	eine Arbeit korrigieren
register [ˈredʒɪstə]	Klassenbuch; Namenliste
order mark	*etwa:* Eintrag ins Klassenbuch
to *be suspended [səˈspendɪd]	zeitweilig vom Unterricht ausgeschlossen werden
to *be expelled	von der Schule 'fliegen'
to skip (a lesson)	(eine Unterrichtsstunde) schwänzen
to *be cancelled	*hier:* ausfallen, gestrichen sein
excursion [ɪkˈskɜːʃn]	Exkursion, Ausflug (mit Bus oder Bahn)
day out	Ausflug, Wandertag
to *be at a school	an einer Schule sein
school leaving certificate [səˈtɪfɪkət]	Schulabschlusszeugnis
to *do written exams	schriftliche Prüfungen machen
form captain [ˈkæptɪn]	(von Mitschüler/innen gewählte/r) Klassensprecher/in
school leaving exams	Abschlussprüfung
to drop (a subject)	(ein Fach) abwählen
main subject	Hauptfach, *hier:* Leistungskurs

Relationships and problems

1   Members of the family

Linda: There's a party at Alan's house on Saturday. Are you going?

Sue: I can't! It's my parents' silver wedding, and they want all the family to be there. We've got so many relations! My grandparents are coming, and all my aunts and uncles. Even my great-grandmother will be there! She's coming with her daughter – that's my great-aunt! She's my godmother, too.

Linda: And any younger members of the family?

Sue: Oh yes, it won't be just the older generation! My cousins Mark and Jenny are coming. You know – the twins. They're fifteen now. My baby nephew Ben will be the youngest!

Linda: You never told me you had a nephew!

Sue: Yes, my half-sister Lesley's son. Lesley is ten years older than me. She got married last year, don't you remember?

Linda: Oh yes! Doesn't her husband come from Denmark?

Sue: No, Sweden! So I've got a Swedish brother-in-law!

Linda: I didn't know Lesley was your half-sister.

Sue: Yes, my father was married before. Lesley is his daughter from his first marriage. My mother is his second wife. So she's *my* real mother – and Lesley's stepmother.

Linda: It all sounds very complicated! But it must be nice to have all those relations. My mother and father haven't got any brothers and sisters – and I'm an only child, too.

member of the family	Familienmitglied
wedding	Hochzeit
relation to *be related to s.o.	Verwandte/r mit jdm verwandt sein
grandparents	Großeltern
grandmother/grandma;	Großmutter/Oma;
grandfather/grandpa	Großvater/Opa
aunt [ɑːnt]	Tante
uncle [ˈʌŋkl]	Onkel
great-grandmother	Urgroßmutter
great-grandfather	Urgroßvater
great-aunt	Großtante
godmother godfather	Patentante Patenonkel
generation [ˌdʒenəˈreɪʃn]	Generation
cousin [ˈkʌzn]	Cousin, Cousine
twins	Zwillinge
nephew [ˈnevjuː] niece [niːs]	Neffe Nichte
half-sister half-brother	Halbschwester Halbbruder
to *get married	heiraten
husband	Ehemann
brother-in-law sister-in-law;	Schwager Schwägerin;
mother-in-law; father-in-law	Schwiegermutter; Schwiegervater
married	verheiratet
marriage [ˈmærɪdʒ]	Ehe
wife	Ehefrau
stepmother stepfather;	Stiefmutter Stiefvater;
stepsister; stepbrother	Stiefschwester; Stiefbruder
brothers and sisters	Geschwister
an only child	ein Einzelkind

2   Taken from the Problem Page

Dear Debbie,

Please help me! I haven't got a boyfriend, but I'm crazy about a boy who lives in our road. I met him at a party – and it was love at first sight! I'd like to ask him for a date, but I'm too shy. I don't think he's going out with anyone else. I'd be heart-broken if he was! How can I make him fall in love with me?

Kim (15)

Dear Debbie,

What can I do about my mother? My parents are divorced, so I'm part of a one-parent family. Now my mother has started a new relationship, and she wants her new partner to move in with us! He is separated, but he's got two children – and they're awful!! I've tried to talk to my mother, but she says it's none of my business.

Unhappy (16)

3   Can you do without it?

Addiction can take many forms. The alcoholic is addicted to alcohol, the drug addict can't stop taking drugs. But there are other substances that seem less harmful, such as the nicotine in cigarettes, or even the caffeine in coffee, which can cause problems if they are taken to excess.

Marian: My mother always told me not to smoke, but I wanted to try it out – like my friends! It started as a kind of rebellion against authority, but then I found I couldn't stop. I'm glad I've given it up now! These days I always look for the non-smoking areas in restaurants, and I must say, I feel much healthier altogether.

boyfriend girlfriend	fester Freund feste Freundin
to *be crazy about s.o./s.th.	verrückt sein nach jdm/etwas
to *meet s.o.	jdm begegnen
love at first sight	Liebe auf den ersten Blick
date to date s.o. *(AE)*	Rendezvous mit jdm ausgehen
shy	schüchtern
to *go out with s.o. *(BE)*	mit jdm (aus)gehen
heart-broken [hɑːt] heart	untröstlich Herz
to *fall in love (with s.o.)	sich verlieben (in jdn)
divorced [dɪˈvɔːst] divorce	geschieden Scheidung
one-parent family	Familie mit einem allein erziehenden Elternteil
relationship	Beziehung
partner	Partner/in
to move in with s.o.	zu jdm ziehen
separated [ˈsepəreɪtɪd] separation	getrennt Trennung
awful	schrecklich
It's none of my business [ˈbɪznɪs]	Es geht mich nichts an.
to *do without s.th.	ohne etwas auskommen, auf etwas verzichten
addiction [əˈdɪkʃn]	Sucht, Süchtigkeit
alcoholic	Alkoholiker/in
alcoholism [ˈælkəhɒlɪzəm]	Alkoholismus
drug addict [ˈædɪkt]	Drogensüchtige/r
to *take drugs	Drogen nehmen
substance [ˈsʌbstəns]	Stoff
harmful	schädigend, schädlich
nicotine [ˈnɪkətiːn]	Nikotin
cigarette [ˌsɪgəˈret]	Zigarette
caffeine [ˈkæfiːn]	Koffein
coffee	Kaffee
to *take s.th. to excess	etwas im Übermaß zu sich nehmen
to smoke	rauchen
to try s.th. out	etwas ausprobieren
rebellion [rɪˈbeljən]	Aufstand, Rebellion
to rebel against s.th.	rebellieren gegen etwas
authority	*hier:* Autorität
to *give s.th. up	mit etwas aufhören, etwas aufgeben
non-smoking area [ˈeərɪə]	Nichtraucherzone, rauchfreie Zone
healthy health	gesund Gesundheit

John: I usually only smoke at parties. I've never taken drugs. But when I was about thirteen, I tried glue-sniffing with a friend. Then his mother caught us and told us off! Luckily my parents never got to know about it. I've only been drunk once, but that was enough, I had such a terrible hangover. It was embarrassing, too, as I was staying at a friend's house, and I was sick all over the carpet!

Sally: How awful! The only thing I've ever been addicted to is spending money. Mostly on clothes! I used to think I'd be more popular if I followed the latest trends. Of course, everyone wants to feel accepted. But now I think it's a bit childish if everyone always tries to keep up with everyone else.

Mike: You're right, it *is* childish! After all, real friends accept you for your personality and your values, not for your appearance. Whenever I start to feel inferior because of what I'm wearing (or *not* wearing!), I try to ignore the feeling – and stop worrying!

4   Trouble at home

Here are some of the things that so often cause trouble, unhappiness – and arguments! – in the family ...

Sam: I can't talk things over properly with my parents. When something goes wrong, they're never prepared to have a discussion about it. They always think they're right and I'm wrong. Then they blame me if I blow up! But I don't apologize. Why should I?

glue-sniffing [glu:]	(Klebstoff) schnüffeln
to *catch s.o. (doing s.th.)	jdn bei etwas erwischen, ertappen
to *tell s.o. off (for doing s.th.)	jdn (wegen etwas) ausschimpfen, schelten
to *get to know about s.th.	etwas herausfinden, von etwas hören
drunk	betrunken
hangover ['‒‚‒ ‒]	Kater
embarrassing	peinlich
to *be sick	sich übergeben
to *spend money	Geld ausgeben
popular ['pɒpjʊlə]	beliebt
trend	Mode, Trend
accepted	angenommen, akzeptiert
childish	kindisch
to *keep up with s.o.	mit jdm Schritt halten, mithalten können
personality [‚‒ ‒'‒ ‒ ‒]	Persönlichkeit
values	Werte
appearance	Erscheinung, Aussehen
inferior [ɪn'fɪərɪə]	unterlegen, minderwertig
to ignore	übergehen, nicht beachten
to worry	sich Sorgen machen
trouble	Ärger, Schwierigkeiten
argument ['ɑːgjʊmənt] to argue	Auseinandersetzung sich streiten
to talk things over with s.o.	Dinge besprechen, bereden
to *go wrong	schief laufen
to *be prepared to do s.th.	bereit sein, etwas zu tun
discussion [dɪ'skʌʃn] to discuss	Diskussion, Streitgespräch besprechen
to blame [bleɪm] s.o. (for s.th.)	jdn beschuldigen, jdm die Schuld geben
to *blow up	explodieren, in die Luft gehen
to apologize [ə'pɒlədʒaɪz] an apology	sich entschuldigen eine Entschuldigung

Judy: My mother always criticizes me a lot. I hate that. She always complains about everything. One day she doesn't approve of my hairstyle, and the next day it's my behaviour at home, or my social life. Then she accuses me of being selfish – or not making an effort at school. Sometimes I feel so rebellious, I want to leave home altogether and live my own life as an independent adult. Then at least I could do as I please.

Robin: I sometimes feel depressed or bad-tempered when I get up. My father gets impatient then. He can't stand bad moods! I suppose it's natural for parents to get annoyed, too, sometimes. After all, they bring you up and do what they think best. But I think they should respect you more – and treat you more like a grown-up.

Liz: I normally get on well with my parents. They're very fond of me, and they aren't strict at all. They give me enough pocket money, too, and lots of privileges. But I sometimes feel I can't live up to their expectations. This puts me under pressure quite a bit. I sometimes even think it would be easier if they didn't care about me so much!

Paul: My mum worries all the time, especially if I'm out late at night. She says she's responsible for me and all that. But I think it's important for people my age to learn to look after themselves. Parents ought to trust their children more, instead of always expecting the worst!

"Blow out the candles and make a wish: we've already made ours."

to criticize ['krɪtɪsaɪz] criticism	kritisieren Kritik
to hate	hassen
to complain about s.th./s.o.	sich über etwas/jdn beschweren, beklagen
to approve of s.th.	etwas gutheißen, für gut halten
hairstyle	Frisur
behaviour [bɪ'heɪvjə] to behave	Verhalten sich benehmen
social ['səʊʃl] life	Freizeitgestaltung mit Freunden
to accuse s.o. of doing s.th.	jdn beschuldigen, etwas getan zu haben
selfish	selbstsüchtig, egoistisch
to *make an effort	sich bemühen, anstrengen
rebellious [rɪ'beljəs]	rebellisch, widerspenstig
to *leave home	von zu Hause weggehen, ausziehen
to live your own life	das eigene Leben führen
independent	unabhängig, selbständig
adult ['ædʌlt] (noun/adj.)	Erwachsene/r, erwachsen
to *do as you please	tun, was einem gefällt/passt
depressed	deprimiert, niedergeschlagen
to *be bad-tempered	schlechte Laune haben
impatient [ɪm'peɪʃnt]	ungeduldig
he can't stand s.th./s.o.	er kann etwas/jdn nicht ausstehen
mood	Laune
to *get annoyed	sich ärgern, sich aufregen
to *bring s.o. up	jdn großziehen, aufziehen
to *do what you think best	tun, was man für das Beste hält
to respect	achten, respektieren
to treat	behandeln
grown-up (noun/adj.)	Erwachsene/r, erwachsen
to *get on well with s.o.	mit jdm gut auskommen
to *be fond of s.o./s.th.	jdn/etwas mögen, gern haben
to *be strict	streng sein
pocket money	Taschengeld
privilege ['prɪvɪlɪdʒ]	Sonderrecht, Privileg
to live up to s.th.	etwas gerecht werden (Erwartungen, Anforderungen)
expectation [ˌekspek'teɪʃn]	Erwartung
to *put s.o. under pressure ['preʃə]	jdn unter Druck setzen
to care about s.o.	hier: sich um jdn sorgen/jdn lieben
to *be responsible [rɪ'spɒnsəbl] for s.th.	verantwortlich sein für etwas
to look after oneself	selbst auf sich aufpassen
to trust s.o.	jdm vertrauen

Young people's interests

1   The generation gap – is this something new?

Last week we asked for your comments on the generation gap and said that we would publish the best 'father/son' and 'mother/daughter' letter in our next issue. Here are our choices:

FATHER'S VIEW:

My son says I don't understand him. My father didn't understand me, either! The generation gap is nothing new. My father had done very different things in his spare time 'when he was a boy' – but his interests and hobbies held no attraction for me: collecting stamps, cycling, hiking through the countryside, even dancing!
   My generation's ideas of leisure activities were things like hitch-hiking to Turkey and back, journeys to Spain or North Africa in our summer holidays (student hostels, of course: camping was something for the boy scouts of my father's generation). We did the 'twist' at parties and, later, discos, and went on trips to open-air concerts. We also did a lot more sport at school than today's kids!

SON'S OPINION:

When my father talks about sport he means team games like soccer, rugby, cricket, hockey and, of course, athletics. My generation thinks of individual pursuits like windsurfing, skateboarding, hang-gliding and parascending. The more energetic of his friends joined tennis or squash clubs in those days. For us a game of billiards or snooker at the youth club on Friday night is hard enough.

MOTHER ...

When I was younger I loved the theatre, and took part in a lot of ama-teur productions and performances of sometimes quite avant-garde plays. But these were usually performed with the help of the school orchestra on the school stage. And of course they were for an audience of parents or friends who did not criticize our acting. As for music, we thought we were really 'with it' when we were young!

generation [ˌdʒenəˈreɪʃn] gap gap	Generationskonflikt Lücke
spare time	Freizeit
interest to *be interested in s.th.	Interesse sich für etwas interessieren
attraction [əˈtrækʃn]	Anziehungskraft, Attraktion
collecting stamps	Briefmarkensammeln
cycling	Radfahren
hiking [ˈhaɪkɪŋ] to hike	Wandern wandern
countryside	Landschaft
dancing to dance	Tanzen tanzen
leisure [ˈleʒə] activity	Freizeitaktivität
hitch-hiking	trampen
journey	Reise
camping	Zelten
boy scout [skaʊt] girl guide	Pfadfinder Pfadfinderin
party	Fest, Feier, Party
trip	Ausflug, Reise
open-air concert	Freiluftkonzert
team game	Mannschaftsspiel
soccer [ˈsɒkə] (AsSOCiation football)	Fußball
rugby [ʌ]	Rugby
cricket [ˈkrɪkɪt]	Kricket
athletics [æθˈletɪks]	Leichtathletik
pursuit [pəˈsjuːt]	Beschäftigung, Zeitvertreib
windsurfing	Windsurfen
skateboarding	Skateboard fahren
hang-gliding	Drachenfliegen
parascending	Fallschirmsport
energetic [ˌenəˈdʒetɪk]	aktiv
to join a club	Mitglied eines Clubs werden
billiards	Billard
snooker	Pool-Billard, Snooker
theatre [ˈθɪətə]	Theater
to *take part in s.th.	an etwas teilnehmen
production	Inszenierung
performance	Aufführung
play	(Theater-)Stück
to perform	aufführen
orchestra [ˈɔːkɪstrə]	Orchester
stage	Bühne
audience [ˈɔːdɪəns]	Publikum, Zuschauer
acting	schauspielerische Leistung
to *be 'with it' (slang)	voll im Trend sein

... AND DAUGHTER

I sometimes go to the theatre with Mum and Dad, but I prefer going to the cinema. Today's teenagers seem to be a bit more musical than their parents. I play the guitar quite well. I'm even in the school rock band. Not so many people of my parents's generation seem to play an instrument or make their own music nowadays. I listen to music on my walkman all the time – except at school, of course!

2   Don't just stand there – join your local leisure centre!

Are you an active sportsman or sportswoman?
Would you just like to get fit and stay fit?
Or are you more interested in meeting old friends or making new ones?
Why not join your local leisure centre?

We offer a wide range of indoor and outdoor games and sports: from badminton, basketball, boxing, football, judo, tennis, volleyball to mountaineering and rock-climbing. Or what about learning to sail?

Our athletics teams regularly take part in competitions. And our athletes have won many individual prizes. Perhaps you are interested in American games? We can even offer beginners' courses in American football and baseball.

Our experienced coaches and instructors will show you how to get the most out of your kind of sport. We also organize visits to sports facilities which we do not have here for members who want to go ice-skating, sailing, skiing, or to do water sports like scuba-diving and canoeing. But we believe that amateur sport should be more than a challenge, it should be fun. Our teams play to win but they play fair. If we lose a match or do badly in a tournament we blame ourselves, not the referee or the umpire.

But it's not all sport. Our leisure centre organizes other activities: theatre or cinema visits and bridge or whist parties for people who enjoy playing cards; painting and drawing courses for all age groups; keep fit sessions and 'gentle jogging' for the over-60s.

cinema ['sɪnəmə]	Kino
to play an instrument ['– – –]	ein Instrument spielen
to *make music	Musik machen
musician [mjuːˈzɪʃn]	Musiker/in
leisure ['leʒə] **centre**	Freizeitzentrum
sportsman, sportswoman	Sportler/in
to *meet friends	sich mit Freunden treffen
to *make friends	Freundschaften schließen
indoor and outdoor sports	Hallen- und Freiluftsportarten
judo ['dʒuːdəʊ]	Judo
mountaineering	Bergsteigen
rock-climbing	Klettern
to *learn to do s.th.	lernen, etwas zu tun
to sail sailing	segeln Segeln
team	Mannschaft
competition to compete (in)	Wettbewerb teilnehmen (an)
athlete ['æθliːt]	Leichtathlet/in
prize [praɪz]	Preis *(Gewinn)*
course	Kurs
experienced	erfahren
coach to coach s.o.	Coach, Trainer/in jdn trainieren
instructor	Lehrer/in
facility [–'– – –]	Einrichtung
ice-skating	Eislaufen
skiing	Skilaufen
water sports	Wassersport
scuba-diving ['skuːbəˌdaɪvɪŋ]	Sporttauchen
canoeing [kəˈnuːɪŋ]	Kanufahren
challenge	Herausforderung
to *be fun	Spaß machen
to *win	gewinnen
to play fair	fair spielen
to *lose	verlieren
match	Spiel, Match
tournament	Tournier
referee [ˌrefəˈriː] *(football, rugby)*	Schiedsrichter/in
umpire ['ʌmpaɪə] *(tennis, cricket)*	Schiedsrichter/in
bridge/whist	Bridge-/Whistspiel (Kartenspiele)
to play cards	Karten spielen
to paint	malen
to *draw	zeichnen
keep fit	Fitness
session	Stunde, 'Sitzung'

3   Holiday plans

Geoff: What are your plans for the summer holidays, Patrick?

Patrick: I'm not going on holiday. I'm saving up for a new computer.

Geoff: What's wrong with your old one? You've got everything: hard disk, modem, mouse, joystick and a modern keyboard.

Patrick: The CPU – that's the central processing unit – is far too slow. And I'd also like a CD-ROM drive and a proper flat-bed scanner – I've only got a hand scanner at the moment. I need a colour printer, too.

Geoff: What do you need all that hardware for? I thought you were only interested in computer games.

Patrick: Computer games are for kids. I want to start scanning photographs in colour. I've got a pirate copy of some picture-processing software. The only problem is that picture documents contain huge amounts of data and take up a lot of memory capacity. My tired old computer is OK for word processing, but it can't process big files of picture data.

Geoff: But last week you said you wanted to save up for a portable computer – a notebook.

Patrick: That was last week – But what are you doing this summer, Geoff? Are you going youth hostelling again?

Geoff: I want to get a summer job at a holiday camp. A friend of mine had a wonderful time at Butlins last year. In the evenings he played the guitar and sang as a part of the entertainment programme for adults, and during the morning he helped organize the amusement arcade for the kids. There was a funfair, a pub and even a zoo. All the rides were free. And he had plenty of free time in the afternoons, except when they organized treasure hunts or picnics and barbecues for the younger kids.

Patrick: Do you think I could get a job there, too?

Geoff: You could try. I'll give you the address.

to save up for s.th.	für etwas sparen
hard disk	Festplatte
modem ['məʊdem]	Modem
mouse	Maus
keyboard	Tastatur
CPU (central processing unit)	zentrale Verarbeitungseinheit
CD-ROM drive	CD-ROM-Laufwerk
flat-bed scanner	Flachbett-Scanner
printer	Drucker
hardware	Hardware
pirate copy	Raubkopie
picture-processing software	Bildverarbeitungssoftware
picture document	Bilddokument
data ['deɪtə]	Daten
memory	Speicher(platz)
capacity [kə'pæsətɪ]	Kapazität
word processing	Textverarbeitung
to process ['– –]	verarbeiten
file	Datei
portable ['pɔːtəbl] **computer**	tragbarer Computer
to *go youth hostelling	in Jugendherbergen übernachten
holiday camp	Feriendorf
Butlins	*berühmte Organisation für Ferien-dörfer in GB*
entertainment [,– –'– –]	Unterhaltung
to entertain s.o.	jdn unterhalten
amusement arcade [aː'keɪd]	Spielsalon, -halle
funfair	Kirmes, Jahrmarkt
pub [ʌ]	Gastwirtschaft, Kneipe
zoo [zuː]	Zoo, Tiergarten
ride to *ride	Fahrt (Karussell usw.) reiten, fahren
free time	Freizeit
treasure ['treʒə] **hunt**	Schatzsuche
picnic	Picknick
barbecue ['baːbɪkjuː]	Grillfest
to barbecue	grillen

The world of work

1 Situations vacant

Experienced SECRETARY needed for well-known local firm of accountants. Applications in handwriting please to Ms Irene Smith, JOHNSON, TURNER & WHITE, Town Square, Buxton DY16 9UW.

SMITH'S BOOKSHOP
has a vacancy for an intelligent shop assistant. Full on-the-job training and good working conditions.

NO SUCCESS WITH JOB APPLICATIONS?
Have you tried your local JOBCENTRE? We have all the latest job offers. Our careers service can even help people with few qualifications. Or why not get your qualifications through YTS?
Phone for a personal interview with one of our careers officers: 081 653 7560.

WANTED gardener and painter and decorator for small hotel: Ring (061) 536 0421.

Share in our success.
Are you under 20 and tired of working on an assembly line?
We still have two vacancies for skilled workers in our newly-opened factory. Previous experience in engineering an advantage. Box 2296.

Interested in money?
The National Westminster Bank is looking for young people who would like to train for a career in banking. Earn good money while you learn about the world of finance. You will find a pleasant atmosphere and friendly colleagues at our banks. Ask the manager of any NATWEST branch for full details.

THIRD-WORLD AID
Our organization needs teachers, doctors, nurses and engineers who want to work in a developing country for at least a year. All applicants should be under 30. Ring Jill Adams on (0256) 167097 for details.

situations vacant ['veɪkənt]	Stellenangebote, freie Stellen
situation	Stellenangebot
experienced	erfahren
to *have experience	Erfahrung haben
secretary ['sekrətrɪ]	Sekretär/in
firm	Firma
accountant [ə'kaʊntənt]	Steuerberater/in, Buchhalter/in
application	Bewerbung
vacancy ['veɪkənsɪ]	freie Stelle
shop assistant	Verkäufer/in
on-the-job training	Ausbildung während der Arbeit
working conditions	Arbeitsbedingungen
success to succeed	Erfolg Erfolg haben
Jobcentre	Arbeitsamt
offer to offer	Angebot anbieten
careers [kə'rɪəz] **service**	Berufsberatung des Jobcentre
qualification [ˌkwɒlɪfɪ'keɪʃn]	Qualifikation
YTS (= Youth Training Scheme)	berufliches Ausbildungsprogramm für Jugendliche
interview ['ɪntəvjuː]	hier: (Beratungs-)Gespräch
careers [kə'rɪəz] **officer**	Berufsberater/in
gardener	Gärtner/in
painter and decorator	Maler/in und Innendekorateur/in
to share in s.th.	hier: an etwas teilnehmen
assembly [ə'semblɪ] **line**	Fließband
skilled worker	(gelernte/r) Facharbeiter/in
factory	Fabrik
previous ['priːvjəs]	vorherig
engineering [ˌendʒɪ'nɪərɪŋ]	Maschinenbau
advantage disadvantage	Vorteil Nachteil
to train for s.th.	sich für etwas ausbilden lassen
career [kə'rɪə]	Laufbahn, Karriere, Beruf
banking	Bankwesen
to earn	verdienen
finance ['– –]	Finanzwesen
colleague ['kɒliːg]	Kollege, Kollegin
bank manager	Filialleiter/in einer Bank
branch	Filiale, Zweigstelle
doctor	Arzt/Ärztin
nurse male nurse	Krankenschwester Krankenpfleger
engineer [ˌendʒɪ'nɪə]	Ingenieur/in
applicant	Bewerber/in

2   Finding a job

Finding any job is difficult today. It is also important to find the right
job. Some young people enjoy talking to people, answering the phone,
listening to people's problems. Some are happier working in an office,
typing letters, working with cars or machines, installing or repairing
equipment. Others become nurses or veterinary nurses because they
want to help people or animals. There are plenty of jobs for social
workers who would like to look after old people, children or the
disabled.

You need certain skills for most jobs, but these skills are not always
so specialized. A nurse or hairdresser should be able to get on with
people. A painter and decorator needs more creativity than a bus driver
or a taxi driver, but a taxi driver needs a better memory. A builder must
be handy with tools but he or she does not need to have the same read-
ing and writing skills as a civil servant, a translator or an interpreter!

Some jobs require A-Levels or higher qualifications: doctors, den-
tists and vets, of course, but also pilots, editors and so on.

Most beginners in any job will need to follow instructions. Many
manual workers have to work outdoors in all weathers, but a surprising
number of 'indoor' jobs include some outdoor work. So the first ques-
tion you should ask yourself is: Do I like working indoors or outdoors?
Then look at the jobs on the lists.

Indoors

Electrician	Photographer
Engineer	Programmer
Flight attendant	Receptionist
Journalist/Reporter	Travel agent
Mechanic	

Outdoors

Customs officer	Miner
Docker	Police officer
Farmer	Postman/postwoman
Firefighter	Sailor
Fisherman	Soldier
Lorry driver	Traffic warden

to type [taɪp]	tippen, Maschine schreiben
to install [ɔ:]	installieren
to repair s.th.	etwas reparieren
equipment [ɪˈkwɪpmənt] *(singular only)*	Geräte
veterinary [ˈvetərɪnərɪ] **nurse**	Tierarzthelfer/in
social worker	Sozialarbeiter/in
the disabled	Behinderte (als Gruppe)
skill	Fertigkeit
hairdresser	Friseur, Friseuse
to *get on with s.o.	mit jdm gut auskommen
creativity [‚– –ˈ– – –]	Kreativität, schöpferische Phantasie
builder	Bauarbeiter/in
handy with tools	handwerklich geschickt
civil [sɪvl] **servant**	Beamter/Beamtin
translator	Übersetzer/in
interpreter	Dolmetscher/in
dentist	Zahnarzt, -ärztin
vet	Tierarzt, -ärztin
pilot [ˈpaɪlət]	Pilot/in
editor	Redakteur/in
to follow instructions	Anweisungen befolgen
manual [ˈ– –] **worker**	Handwerker/in
outdoors indoors	im Freien, draußen drinnen
electrician	Elektriker/in
flight attendant	Flugbegleiter/in
journalist; reporter	Journalist/in; Reporter/in
mechanic [mɪˈkænɪk]	KFZ-Mechaniker/in
photographer [‚–ˈ– – –]	Fotograf/in
programmer	Programmierer/in
receptionist	Empfangsdame/-herr
travel agent	Reisebüroangestellte/r
customs officer	Zollbeamter/-beamtin
docker	Hafenarbeiter/in
farmer	Bauer/Bäuerin, Landwirt/in
firefighter	Feuerwehrmann/-frau
fisherman	Fischer
miner	Bergarbeiter/in
police officer	Polizist/in
postman/postwoman	Postbote, Postbotin
sailor	Seemann (Männer u. Frauen)
soldier	Soldat/in
traffic warden	Verkehrspolizist/in, Politesse

3 A talk with the school careers teacher

Ms Hart: Come in, Adrian ... Let me see: you're interested in a career in banking.

Adrian: That's right, Ms Hart.

Ms Hart: Employers – especially banks – like their employees to have good marks in English and Maths, which should not be a problem for you. Now, if you want to start after the summer holidays you should apply for a job now. I saw an advertisement in the *Chronicle* last week. The National Westminster Bank is looking for trainees. If they take you, you'll have a six-month trial period. So you'll be able to find out if you like the job – and if the job likes you. Your income wouldn't be very high to start with – the salary for a trainee bank clerk is about £6,000 a year ...

Adrian: Oh ...

Ms Hart: ... but you get a rise regularly – banks usually increase their employees' wages every year. And the chances of promotion are quite good, too. The brightest people are often promoted to branch manager while they're still in their thirties.

Adrian: I'm only sixteen ...

Ms Hart: I know, Adrian. But banking is a profession, and professional people have to think ahead. Why are you specially interested in banking?

Adrian: Well, it's a steady job with good prospects – you don't often hear of bank clerks on the dole.

Ms Hart: That's true. But some banks are open on Saturday mornings nowadays. Banking is one of the few office jobs where you might have to work on Saturday morning. But you only have a seven-hour working day, and you get one afternoon off during the week. And you don't have to do overtime or shift work. You should write your letter of application right away, Adrian.

careers [kə'rɪəz] **teacher**	Lehrer/in, der/die für die Berufs-
	beratung zuständig ist
employer [–'– –]	Arbeitgeber/in
employee [ˌ– –'–]	Arbeitnehmer/in
to apply for a job	sich um eine Stelle bewerben
advertisement [əd'vɜ:tɪsmənt]	Anzeige
trainee [–'–]	Auszubildende/r, Azubi
trial period	Probezeit
income	Einkommen
salary ['– – –]	Gehalt (wird monatlich bezahlt)
bank clerk	Bankangestellte/r
to *get a rise	eine Gehaltserhöhung bekommen
to increase [–'–]	erhöhen
wages	Lohn (allgemein, auch Wochenlohn)
promotion [–'– –]	Beförderung
bright	intelligent, 'hell'
to promote s.o.	jdn befördern
branch manager	Zweigstellenleiter/in
profession	Beruf, der eine höhere Ausbildung
	erfordert
professional people	Berufsprofis, Professionelle
to *think ahead	an die Zukunft denken
a steady job	ein sicherer Arbeitsplatz
prospects	Aussichten
to *be on the dole	arbeitslos sein
office job	Büroarbeit
working day	Arbeitstag
an afternoon/a morning off	ein freier Nach-/Vormittag
to *do overtime	Überstunden machen
to *do shift work	Schichtarbeit machen
letter of application	Bewerbung(sschreiben)

A school-leaver was being interviewed for a job.
"You'll get fifty pounds a week to begin with," said the manager,
"and then after six months you'll get seventy pounds a week."
"Fine," said the school-leaver, "I'll come back in six months!"

4   A letter of application

36 Walmsley Grove
Urmston
Manchester M21 6PE

WILSON ENGINEERING Co. Ltd.
Personnel Dept.
Flag Lane
Crewe ST6 9UW

16th April 1994

Re: Your advertisement offering engineering apprenticeships

Dear Sir/Madam,

I am 16 years old and left school last year with 3 GCSE passes (English, Maths and Technical Drawing). I would like to apply for one of your engineering apprenticeships.

As there were no vacancies for engineering apprentices in my area at the time, I tried to find a full-time job in a local firm. But as unemployment is high in our part of Manchester, and I was unable to find anything, I decided to go to technical college. I also took a part-time job (evenings only) at a small toy factory, to get some work experience and to improve my technical ability.

Please let me know whether you are able to consider me for an apprenticeship. I can send the usual references and am enclosing my CV and a photocopy of my GCSE certificate. I am also sending you a copy of a short article from our local paper about the factory where I am working at the moment.

Yours faithfully,   Patricia Andrews

VERY SPECIAL FACTORY – Self-help project in Urmston

This toy factory in Urmston is run by unemployed people from the area. Most of them are skilled workers who were made redundant when a big local toy factory closed down after a long strike last year.

Workers went on strike for better working conditions (the firm had a reputation for firing members of the trade unions).

Some of the workers at this small, self-help factory have been out of work and on unemployment benefit for long periods. The manager is Mr Joe Collins, who retired from the old company last year.

Co. (= **Co**mpany) [ˈkʌmpənɪ]	Firma, Gesellschaft
Ltd. (= **Limited**)	*etwa:* GmbH
personnel dept. (= **dep**artment)	Personalabteilung
re: [riː] (= **referring to**)	Betr., bezüglich
apprenticeship [–ʹ– – –]	Lehre
apprentice	Lehrling, Auszubildende/r
full-time job	Vollzeitbeschäftigung, Ganztagsstelle
unemployment	Arbeitslosigkeit
technical college	technische Fachhochschule
part-time job	Teilzeitstelle
work experience	Arbeitserfahrung
technical ability	technisches Können
reference	*hier:* Empfehlung
to enclose	beilegen
CV (= **c**urriculum **v**itae)	Lebenslauf
photocopy [ʹ– –, – –]	Fotokopie
certificate [səʹtɪfɪkət]	Prüfungszeugnis
self-help	Selbsthilfe
to *run a firm	eine Firma führen, leiten
unemployed	arbeitslos
to *be made redundant [–ʹ– –]	den Arbeitsplatz verlieren, arbeitslos werden
to close down	schließen (Werk, Fabrik)
strike	Streik
to *go on strike/to strike	streiken
reputation	Ruf
to fire s.o.	jdn feuern
trade union [ʹjuːnjən]	Gewerkschaft
to *be out of work	arbeitslos sein
to *be on unemployment benefit	Arbeitslosengeld beziehen
manager	Geschäftsführer/in
to retire	sich zur Ruhe setzen, in Rente gehen
retired	pensioniert

> – *How many people work in this office?*
> – *About half of them.*

Way of life

1 Are you OK?

Everybody wants to be happy. But is happiness still possible in our hectic modern society? Here are two opinions:

Sarah (19): Life these days is very competitive. There's a lot of pressure to do well. I suppose everyone is afraid of failure. You just have to work hard if you want to be successful. First you must have a goal, of course, and then do all you can to achieve it! Personally, I feel happiest when I'm working – so I don't mind the stress. It's become a habit now.

David (22): Nearly everyone seems to be in a hurry. Some people are so busy, they have no time to relax and enjoy life. But you can work out an alternative lifestyle if you really want to. Wealth isn't so important to me. I don't need to fly to exotic countries when I go on holiday. A week walking in the hills near home is much more peaceful. And it's cheaper and safer, too! It's best to be satisfied with a simple way of life, I think. Some people are always dreaming of an ideal life in the future. But they spend so much time searching for things they haven't got, they don't notice all the positive aspects of what they have got!

2 Do you really need it?

We are all consumers. But what – and how much – we consume depends, more than you might think, on advertising.

   Advertising is so much a part of our lives that we don't often stop to think what it does to us. What is the aim of all those advertisements, special offers, TV commercials and slogans? To sell things, of course. But it is more than that. It is also to make people buy things that they cannot afford. It is to persuade them to spend their money instead of saving it for more important things. It is to make them dissatisfied with themselves. The message is simple:

"All the best people have got it, so you must have it, too."

way of life	Lebensstil, Lebensart, Lebensweise
happiness	Zufriedenheit, Glück
hectic	hektisch
society	Gesellschaft
competitive [kəm'petɪtɪv]	vom Konkurrenzdenken geprägt
pressure ['preʃə]	Druck
failure ['feɪljə]	Scheitern, Versagen, Misserfolg
successful	erfolgreich
goal [gəʊl]	Ziel
to achieve s.th.	etwas erreichen, erlangen
stress stressful	Stress stressig
habit	Gewohnheit
to *be in a hurry	es eilig haben
busy	beschäftigt
to relax	(sich) entspannen, ausruhen
to enjoy (life)	(das Leben) genießen
alternative [ɔːl'tɜːnətɪv]	Alternativ-
lifestyle	Lebensstil
wealth [welθ]	Reichtum, Wohlstand
to *go on holiday	in Urlaub fahren
peaceful	friedlich
cheap	billig
safe	sicher, gefahrlos
to *be satisfied with s.th.	mit etwas zufrieden sein
simple	einfach, schlicht
to *dream of s.th.	von etwas träumen
future	Zukunft
to *spend (time)	(Zeit) verbringen
to search for s.th.	nach etwas suchen
positive aspect	positive Seite, positiver Aspekt
consumer to consume	Verbraucher/in verbrauchen
advertising ['ædvətaɪzɪŋ]	Werbung, Reklame
aim	*hier:* Zweck
advertisement [əd'vɜːtɪsmənt]	(Werbe-)Anzeige
special offer	Sonderangebot
(TV) commercial [kə'mɜːʃl]	Fernsehwerbung, Werbespot
slogan	Slogan, Werbespruch
to afford [ə'fɔːd] **s.th.**	sich etwas leisten
to persuade [pə'sweɪd] **s.o. to do s.th.**	jdn zu etwas überreden
to *spend (money)	(Geld) ausgeben
to save	*hier:* sparen
dissatisfied	unzufrieden
message ['mesɪdʒ]	Botschaft

3   Women at work – and at home

How emancipated are you? Answer these questions to find out!	Yes	No	Not sure
1. Would you call yourself a feminist?			
2. Do you think it is important to give girls and boys equal opportunities at school – and later at work?			
3. Is it right to bring up children without making any difference between the sexes? (e.g. Would you give a little boy a doll to play with?)			
4. "It is all right for a woman with children to work part-time, but it should be the father's main responsibility to support the family." Is this a sexist attitude?			
5. "If both the man and the woman go out to work, the man should do his share of the housework." Do you agree?			
6. Some people think it is unnatural for a woman to want a career or a business of her own. Is this just prejudice?			
7. Housekeeping and looking after small children is a full-time job. Do you agree?			
8. Is it a disadvantage for young children to be cared for by a child-minder or an au pair instead of their mother or father?			
9. Some women don't want to go back to work after they have had a baby. Do you think that looking after the home and family can be as fulfilling as a paid job?			
10. Over 90 % of British nurses are female. Over 90 % of British university professors are male. Is this because women are usually better at certain jobs – and men usually better at others?			

emancipated	emanzipiert
feminist ['– – –]	Feminist/in
equal ['i:kwəl] equality [–'– – –]	gleich Gleichheit
opportunity [ˌɒpə'tju:nətɪ]	Möglichkeit, Chance
to *bring s.o. up	jdn großziehen, aufziehen
difference	Unterschied, Unterscheidung
sexes	Geschlechter
to work part-time	Teilzeit arbeiten
responsibility	Verantwortung, Pflicht
to support the family	die Familie unterhalten, ernähren
sexist	männer-/frauenfeindlich, sexistisch
attitude	Einstellung, Haltung
to *go out to work	arbeiten gehen
to *do one's share of s.th.	seinen Anteil an etwas machen
housework	Hausarbeit
career [kə'rɪə]	Karriere, Beruf
business ['bɪznɪs]	Geschäft, Betrieb
prejudice ['predʒʊdɪs]	Vorurteil
housekeeping	Haushalten
to look after s.o.	sich um jdn kümmern, auf jdn aufpassen
It's a full-time job	Das kann einen rund um die Uhr beschäftigen
disadvantage advantage	Nachteil Vorteil
to care for s.o.	für jdn sorgen
child-minder	Person, die sich gegen Bezahlung um (fremde) Kinder kümmert
au pair	Au-pair-Mädchen/-Junge
to *go back to work	wieder arbeiten gehen, berufstätig sein
to *have a baby	ein Kind bekommen
a fulfilling job	eine Tätigkeit, in der man Erfüllung findet
to fulfill	erfüllen
female ['fi:meɪl]	weiblich
male	männlich

a detached house   two semi-detached houses   a row of terraced houses   a bungalow

4   Housing

In Britain (and America) it is more common to have a house – or a flat – of your own than it is in Germany. Not so many people live in rented accommodation. On the other hand, although they own their homes, people in Britain – and the USA – move house more often than they do in Germany. So there are usually a lot of houses and flats for sale.

5   I believe

In this world full of problems, a belief in God helps many people to feel their lives have a meaning. Whether you are a Muslim, a Buddhist or a Hindu, a Christian or a Jew, your religion can make a big difference to the way you live.

Nancy (17): A lot of people I know only go to church if there's a wedding, a christening or a funeral in the family. I like the morning service at our church, and the lovely hymns, though I don't go every Sunday. I think you can worship God, read the Bible and pray without going to church.

Philip (18): Some of my friends are atheists. I'm not sure yet what I believe, so I suppose I'm an agnostic. The teachings of Christ are fine. But I find it hard to believe in things like heaven and hell. If God exists, why does he allow so much evil in the world he created?

Liz (21): People's actions are more important than what they say they believe. I wouldn't respect a person more just because he or she was a priest – or even the Pope!

John (20): Religion is OK as long as it doesn't get fanatical. People that belong to sects are often the worst. You have to be very careful what church you join.

detached [dɪ'tætʃt] house	Einfamilienhaus, Einzelhaus
semi-detached house	Doppelhaushälfte
row [rəʊ]	Reihe
terraced house	Reihenhaus
bungalow ['bʌŋgələʊ]	Bungalow
flat block of flats	Wohnung Wohnblock
rented accommodation	Mietwohnung, -haus
to own s.th.	etwas besitzen
to move house	umziehen
to *be for sale	zum Verkauf stehen
to believe in s.th.	an etwas glauben
belief	Glaube
meaning	Sinn, Bedeutung
Muslim ['mʊslɪm]	Moslem, Moslime
Buddhist ['bʊdɪst]	Buddhist/in
Hindu	Hindu, Hinduistin
Christian ['krɪstʃən] Christ [kraɪst]	Christ/in Christus
Jew [dʒu:]	Jude, Jüdin
religion [rɪ'lɪdʒən]	Religion, Glaube
to *go to church	in die Kirche gehen
wedding	Hochzeit
christening ['krɪsnɪŋ]	Taufe
funeral ['fju:nərəl]	Beerdigung
service	Gottesdienst
hymn	Kirchenlied
to worship ['wɜ:ʃɪp]	verehren, anbeten
Bible ['baɪbl]	Bibel
to pray [preɪ]	beten
atheist ['eɪθɪɪst]	Atheist/in
agnostic	Agnostiker/in
teachings	Lehre
heaven	Himmel
hell	Hölle
to exist	existieren
evil (noun/adj.)	Böse, Übel; böse, schlecht
to create	erschaffen, schöpfen
priest [pri:st]	Geistlicher
Pope	Papst
fanatical	fanatisch
to belong to s.th.	etwas angehören, zugehörig sein
sect	Sekte
to join	hier: beitreten

6   Travelling

By road

Simon:	Hello, Judy. Did you have a good journey?
Judy:	Not too bad, I suppose. But I couldn't break any speed limits! There was a lot of traffic on the motorway.
Simon:	As usual!
Judy:	There was an awful hold-up near Bristol. It wasn't the rush-hour, so I thought at first there'd been an accident. But one of the lanes was closed because of road works. So I left the motorway at the next exit.
Simon:	Was it better after that?
Judy:	Not much. I don't think I chose a good route. The main roads were nearly as busy as the motorway. For a long time I was behind an enormous lorry, and I couldn't overtake because there were so many bends. Then there was a diversion. I missed the turning to Exeter, too. I didn't see the sign. And then I went the wrong way!
Simon:	Poor you! But you got here safely in the end.
Judy:	Yes, but I think I'll dream of roundabouts and traffic lights tonight. Well, at least I didn't have a breakdown!
Simon:	I'm quite glad I haven't got a driving licence. Going by public transport is much more relaxing.
Judy:	As long as your friends can pick you up whenever you need a lift, eh, Simon?

– What did the traffic lights say to the car?
– Don't look, I'm changing.

By rail: At the station

Clerk:	Who's next in the queue, please?
Passenger:	We are! – Two tickets to Newcastle, please.
Clerk:	Single or return?
Passenger:	Single, please. Which platform does the train leave from?
Clerk:	Platform 4. The next train's due in twenty minutes. I'm afraid you've just missed one.
Passenger:	Oh well, we'll easily catch the next! Is it a through train?
Clerk:	No – change at York. There's a good connection – you only have to wait fifteen minutes.

to travel	reisen
journey	Reise
speed limit	Geschwindigkeitsbegrenzung
traffic	Verkehr
motorway	Autobahn
hold-up	stockender Verkehr
rush-hour	Hauptverkehrszeit, Rushhour
accident	Unfall
lane	*hier:* Fahrspur
road works	Straßenarbeiten, Baustelle
	(auf der Straße)
exit	(Autobahn-)Ausfahrt
route [ru:t]	Route, Strecke
main road	Hauptverkehrsstraße
to *overtake	überholen
bend	Kurve
diversion [daɪ'vɜːʃn]	Umleitung
to miss the turning	eine Abzweigung verpassen
sign	(Verkehrs-)Schild
to *go the wrong way	falsch fahren, sich verfahren
roundabout	Kreisverkehr
traffic lights	Ampel
breakdown	Panne
driving licence ['laɪsens]	Führerschein
public transport	öffentliche Verkehrsmittel
to pick s.o. up	jdn abholen, mitnehmen
lift	*hier:* Mitfahrgelegenheit
to *give s.o. a lift	jdn mitnehmen
by rail	mit der Bahn
station	Bahnhof
queue [kju:]	Warteschlange
ticket	Fahrkarte, Fahrschein
single	einfache Fahrt
return	Hin- und Rückfahrt
platform	Gleis, Bahnsteig
to *be due [dju:]	*hier:* erwartet werden; laut
	Fahrplan ankommen sollen
to miss	verpassen
to *catch (a train)	(einen Zug) kriegen, erreichen
through train	durchgehender Zug,
	Direktverbindung
to change (trains)	umsteigen
connection	Anschluss, Verbindung

By bike

Christine: I'm really looking forward to this trip. I love cycling!
Melissa: So do I. Have you checked your bike yet?
Christine: More or less. I've tested the brakes and the lights, and they
            work OK. The gears are all right, too, and so is the chain.
Melissa: Your back tyre looks a bit flat. You'd better pump it up.
Christine: Can I have your bicycle pump? My brother took mine – and
            he hasn't given it back yet. And he took some things out of
            my saddlebag, too – to mend a puncture, I think.
Melissa: Here's my pump. – I'm going to change the height of my
            saddle a bit – it's too low. I can pedal better if it's higher.
Christine: Look at my new helmet. What do you think of it?
Melissa: OK – but do we really need helmets? We're going to keep to
            the cycle paths – we won't be riding on any main roads.
Christine: Better to be safe than sorry.
Melissa: That's what my dad always says! But he had a collision
            with a pedestrian and her dog a few weeks ago. The woman
            and the dog were OK, but Dad's front wheel was damaged
            and his handlebars were bent! Luckily it was his old bike –
            not his racing bike.

By air

Mr Körner is a businessman from South Germany. Today he is flying
back to Munich from London. There is a connection by Underground
from central London to Heathrow Airport.

  He gets to the airport in good time, and checks in. He has only got a
small piece of hand luggage, which he can take with him on board the
aircraft. This means he won't have to wait at the baggage reclaim when
he arrives in Munich. He'll be able to go straight to the multi-storey car
park where he's left his car.

cycling cyclist	Radfahren Radfahrer/in
brake	Bremse
to work	*hier:* funktionieren
gear [gɪə] **gears (on a bike)**	Gang Gangschaltung
chain	Kette
tyre	Reifen
to pump a tyre up	einen Reifen aufpumpen
bicycle pump	Fahrradpumpe
saddlebag	Satteltasche
to mend a puncture	einen Reifen flicken
puncture	Reifenpanne, Loch im Reifen
saddle	Sattel
to pedal pedal ['– –]	treten, strampeln Pedal
helmet	Helm
cycle path	Radweg
to *ride (a bicycle)	Rad fahren
collision	Zusammenstoß
to collide	zusammenstoßen
pedestrian	Fußgänger/in
wheel	Rad
to damage ['dæmɪdʒ] **s.th.**	etwas beschädigen
handlebars	Lenkstange
racing bike	Rennrad
Underground	Untergrundbahn
airport	Flughafen
in good time	rechtzeitig; mit genügend Zeit,
to check in	einchecken, sich anmelden
luggage ['lʌgɪdʒ]	Gepäck
on board	an Bord
aircraft	Flugzeug, Maschine
baggage reclaim ['bægɪdʒ rɪ'kleɪm]	Gepäckausgabe
to arrive	ankommen
multi-storey car park	(mehrstöckiges) Parkhaus

He goes up the escalator and looks at the departure board. Sometimes flights are delayed, or – if the weather is really bad – they may even be cancelled. But his flight to Munich is due to leave on schedule.

Mr Körner goes through passport control and security. Then he goes to the departure lounge and waits there for his flight to be called. Soon the gate number is announced. Twenty minutes later the plane is in the air. All seat-belts have been fastened. The captain has spoken a few words over the loud-speaker, and members of the crew are serving a light meal now. They are serving drinks, too. Mr Körner likes a glass of red wine. Cheers!

By sea

Woman:	I'd like some leaflets about ferries to France.
Travel agent:	Where do you want to sail from?
Woman:	Portsmouth, I think. Or is there a shorter crossing to Cherbourg from Weymouth?
Travel agent:	There isn't much difference. – Here are the leaflets – with the timetables and fares. There are details about other destinations, too. Not just Cherbourg.
Woman:	Thanks. – What a lot of interesting catalogues you've got over there. Mediterranean cruises! Trips round the world – fantastic! Those ocean liners look great, don't they?
Travel agent:	They're all right if you like long sea voyages. No good for me. Just the sight of a boat makes me feel seasick!

escalator ['– – – –]	Rolltreppe
departure board	Anzeigetafel der Abflüge
flight to *fly	Flug fliegen
to *be delayed	verspätet sein, Verspätung haben
to cancel s.th.	etwas streichen, absagen, ausfallen lassen
on schedule ['ʃedju:l]	planmäßig, pünktlich
passport control	Passkontrolle
security	Sicherheitskontrolle
departure lounge	Warteraum (vor Abflug)
gate	Ausgang, Flugsteig
to announce s.th.	etwas durchsagen, bekanntgeben
announcement	Durchsage
seat-belt	Sicherheitsgurt
to fasten ['fɑ:sn]	festmachen, schließen
captain	Kapitän
crew	Besatzung, Flugpersonal
ferry	Fähre
travel agent	Reisebürokaufmann, –frau
travel agency	Reisebüro
to sail	abfahren (mit Schiff), absegeln
crossing	Überfahrt
timetable	Fahrplan
fare	Fahrpreis
destination	Reiseziel
catalogue	Katalog
cruise [kru:z]	Kreuzfahrt
trip	Reise, Ausflug
ocean liner ['əʊʃn 'laɪnə]	Ozeandampfer
voyage ['vɔɪdʒ]	Seereise, -fahrt
boat	Boot
seasick	seekrank

Festivities and public holidays

1 Celebrations – in Britain and in Germany

Nicola's German pen-friend, Kathrin, is in England for ten days. It is the end of October, and there are already Christmas decorations in some of the shops.

Nicola: How do you celebrate Christmas in Germany?

Kathrin: The festive season really starts with Advent. Children have Advent calendars, and most people have a wreath with four Advent candles on the table. We bake a lot of biscuits and gingerbread, and a lot of people make things – like decorations or presents.

Nicola: Do German children believe in Father Christmas? Over here they hang up their stockings on Christmas Eve, and Father Christmas comes down the chimney in the night. He fills their stockings with presents, and they open them the next morning – on Christmas Day.

Kathrin: Father Christmas is the same as Santa Claus, isn't he? In Germany we have a similar tradition with Saint Nikolaus. He gives children little presents on December 6th.

Nicola: Do you have Christmas carols? In England it's the custom for carol singers to go round to people's houses in the evenings before Christmas, collecting money for charities.

Kathrin: We do that on January 6th. Children dress up as the Three Kings. You call January 6th Twelfth Night, don't you?

Nicola: Yes, that's right. Is Boxing Day a holiday with you?

Kathrin: Oh yes. And New Year's Day, too. There are a lot of celebrations and parties on New Year's Eve.

Nicola: That's the same here! Dances and balls are popular on New Year's Eve. But even people who don't go out usually stay up till midnight to see the New Year in – and drink a toast.

Kathrin: Do you have fireworks on New Year's Eve, too?

Nicola: No, but we have them on Guy Fawkes Night – that's on November 5th. People have parties outside, usually round a big bonfire, and a home-made 'guy' is burnt on top of it. Some people call Guy Fawkes Night 'Bonfire Night'. You know – Guy Fawkes tried to blow up the Houses of Parliament. At least, he was the one who was caught with all the gunpowder!

festivity [feˈstɪvətɪ], festivities	Feier, Feierlichkeiten
public holiday	gesetzlicher Feiertag
celebration	Feier, Fest
Christmas *(noun/adj.)*	Weihnachten, Weihnachts-
decoration(s) to decorate	Schmuck (z.B. am Baum) schmücken
to celebrate	feiern
festive season	Festzeit
Advent [ˈædvənt]	Advent
wreath [riːθ]	Kranz
candle	Kerze
gingerbread	Gewürzkuchen, Lebkuchen
to *make things	basteln
present	Geschenk
Father Christmas *(BE)*	der Weihnachtsmann
to *hang up one's stocking	den Weihnachtsstrumpf aufhängen, bereitlegen
Christmas Eve	Heiligabend
chimney [ˈtʃɪmnɪ]	Schornstein
Christmas Day	der erste Weihnachtstag
Santa Claus [klɔːz] *(AE)*	der Weihnachtsmann,
saint (St) [seɪnt]	Heilige/r (St.)
Christmas carol	Weihnachtslied
custom [ˈkʌstəm]	Sitte, Brauch
carol [ˈkærəl] singer	Sternsinger
to collect	sammeln
charity [ˈtʃærətɪ]	Wohltätigkeitsverein
to dress up	sich verkleiden
the Three Kings	die Heiligen Drei Könige
Twelfth Night	der 6. Januar (Ende der Weihnachtszeit)
Boxing Day	der zweite Weihnachtstag
New Year's Day	Neujahr, der 1. Januar
New Year's Eve	Silvester
dance	Tanz, Ball
ball [ɔː]	Ball
midnight	Mitternacht
to *see the New Year in	das neue Jahr begrüßen
to *drink a toast (to s.o./s.th.)	(auf jdn/etwas) trinken
fireworks	Feuerwerk
Guy Fawkes [ˌɡaɪˈfɔːks] Night	5. November *(siehe History S. 30)*
bonfire	Feuer, Freudenfeuer
home-made	selbst gebastelt, hausgemacht

2   More holidays and special days

Apart from the usual anniversaries and birthdays that people celebrate every year, there are a number of other special occasions. Some are the same in Britain and in Germany – others are not.

● Valentine's Day (February 14th) is a big day for the makers of greetings cards – it has been a tradition in Britain for over 500 years!

● People eat pancakes on Shrove Tuesday, but there is no equivalent of 'Fasching' in Britain. However, there are sometimes local carnivals with parades through the streets at other times of the year. Fancy dress parties are popular at Halloween (October 31st).

● Lent begins on Ash Wednesday. It is still the custom to 'give up' something during Lent – even if it's only sweets or chocolate! Good Friday is a holiday, and so is Easter Monday. Easter eggs are part of the annual celebrations, but the tradition of the Easter bunny and of painting eggs and hiding them on Easter Day is more common in Germany.

● April Fool's Day is a popular time for practical jokes, and May Day is often celebrated in villages on the first Saturday in May.

● Other church festivals include Whitsun (sometimes also called Pentecost) and Ascension Day. Remembrance Day is the second Sunday in November, when the people who died in the two World Wars are remembered.

● There is no national day in Britain, but in Northern Ireland St Patrick's Day (March 17th) is a public holiday.

● Bank Holidays are days when banks are closed and people don't go to work. They are usually on a Monday – to make a long weekend! The last Mondays in May and August are always Bank Holidays. Boxing Day and Good Friday, although they are church festivals, are also counted as Bank Holidays.

anniversary	Jahrestag
special occasion	besonderer Anlass, Ereignis
Valentine's ['væləntaɪnz] **Day**	Valentinstag
greetings card card	Grußkarte Karte
Shrove [ʃrəʊv] **Tuesday**	Fastnachtsdienstag
equivalent [ɪ'kwɪvələnt]	Entsprechung, Gegenstück
carnival ['kɑːnɪvl]	Karneval
parade [pə'reɪd]	Umzug, Parade
fancy dress	(Masken)kostüm, Verkleidung
Halloween [ˌhæləʊ'iːn]	Tag vor Allerheiligen
Lent	Fastenzeit
Ash Wednesday	Aschermittwoch
Good Friday	Karfreitag
Easter Monday	Ostermontag
Easter egg	Osterei
annual ['ænjʊəl]	jährlich, alljährlich
Easter bunny	Osterhase
Easter Day	Ostersonntag
April Fool's Day	der 1. April
practical joke	Streich
May Day	*gesetzlicher Feiertag am ersten Montag im Mai*
church festival	Kirchenfest
Whitsun ['wɪtsn]	Pfingsten
Pentecost ['pentɪkɒst]	Pfingsten
Ascension [ə'senʃn] **Day**	Himmelfahrt(stag)
Remembrance Day	*britischer Volkstrauertag*
national day	Nationalfeiertag
St Patrick's Day	der 17. März *(irischer Feiertag)*
Bank Holiday	*etwa:* gesetzlicher Feiertag

3   American celebrations

Dear Markus,

In your last letter you asked me to tell you something about holidays in the USA. Well, the biggest day here is the Fourth of July when we celebrate our independence! There are lots of fireworks and parades then.

Thanksgiving Day is important, too. That's when we remember the first Thanksgiving celebrated by the Pilgrims in 1621. It's a big family occasion. Most families have a big get-together, and there's always a big feast – with an enormous turkey to eat!

One of our biggest days for parties is Halloween, which is popular with everyone – not only children! You've probably heard of 'trick or treat'. That's what children say when they come to people's doors dressed up in their Halloween costumes. Sometimes they play really mean tricks if they don't get the treat they want. So it's important to know about the custom if you're new in the States!

We have a few other holidays – for example, Martin Luther King Day, in memory of the great civil rights leader, and Labor Day at the end of the summer vacation.

I needn't tell you much about Christmas over here. But you might be surprised to see our Christmas trees – a lot of people have a plastic tree. Real trees look better, I guess, but it's not bad to have a tree you can put away and use again year after year! (Some people hang up plastic holly and mistletoe, too!)

That's all for now.
All the best,
Nelson

4   What to say on special occasions

 "Happy birthday!"
"Many happy returns of the day!"

"So you've passed your test! Congratulations!"

"Thank you so much for the invitation!"

 "Merry Christmas and a Happy New Year!"

 "Good luck in your exams!"

 "With love and best wishes!"

the Fourth of July	Unabhängigkeitstag (USA)
independence	Unabhängigkeit
independent	unabhängig
Thanksgiving Day	*Feiertag in den USA*
Thanksgiving	Dankfest
the Pilgrims	die Pilgerväter
get-together	Treffen
feast [fiːst]	*hier:* Festessen, Festmahl
turkey ['tɜːkɪ]	Truthahn
trick or treat	*Ausspruch der Kinder zu Halloween*
costume	Kostüm, Verkleidung
to play a trick (on s.o.)	(jdm) einen Streich spielen
mean	gemein, gehässig
treat	etwas Besonderes (oft Süßigkeiten)
Martin Luther King Day	*Feiertag in den USA*
in memory of	zur Erinnerung an, zum Gedenken an
Labor ['leɪbə] Day	*etwa:* Tag der Arbeit
vacation [vəˈkeɪʃn] *(AE)*	Ferien, Urlaub
Christmas tree	Weihnachtsbaum
plastic	Kunststoff
year after year	Jahr für Jahr
holly	Stechpalme (immergrüner Strauch mit roten Beeren)
mistletoe ['mɪsltəʊ]	Mistel
Happy birthday!	Herzlichen Glückwunsch zum Geburts-
Many happy returns of the day!	tag!; Alles Gute zum Geburtstag!
invitation	Einladung
to invite	einladen
Good luck!	Viel Glück!
Congratulations!	Herzlichen Glückwunsch!, ich gratuliere!
Merry Christmas!	Fröhliche Weihnachten!
Happy New Year!	Ein gutes neues Jahr!
With love (from)	Herzlichst (Dein/e)
(With) best wishes	Mit freundlichen Grüßen, mit den besten Wünschen

Features

1 Writing letters

1 Introducing yourself

Dear Sayed,

My name is Karin Müller and I got your address from our English teacher at school. She told me that you wanted to write to a German pen-friend who can speak English. So I'll try not to make any mistakes.

I am 16 years old and live in a small village called Bürg in Southern Germany with my parents and my younger brother Michael. And I go to the technical grammar school in Neuenstadt. But I will be leaving school this summer. I want to become a secretary or a bank clerk if I can get a job in a bank.

My hobbies are music and dancing (we go to a disco in Heilbronn every Saturday), and I also like animals. We have a big black dog called Robin and two cats.

Please write to me soon and tell me something about life in Egypt. I'm really looking forward to hearing from you!

Yours,

Karin Müller

2 A letter to a good friend

Hi there, Karin!

I was so pleased to get your letter. Just a quick note to tell you that your trip to England is OK! Mum and Dad said you could stay with us before we go to Cornwall together.

You talked about pony trekking in your letter. I've got one or two addresses in Wales, but perhaps you should write to the farm where your sister stayed last year. It sounds like a wonderful place! It's on Dartmoor, isn't it?

I'll phone my cousin Cathy and ask her if she'd like to come with us. I hope everything is fine with you. Bye for now and all the best to your parents. Write again soon!

Love,

Samantha

3   Useful phrases for an informal letter

Dear Linda,	Liebe Linda,
Hi (there), John!	Hallo, John!

I was so pleased to get your letter.	Ich habe mich sehr über deinen Brief gefreut.
Thanks for your letter.	Vielen Dank für deinen Brief.

I hope you're well.	
I hope everything is fine with you.	} Ich hoffe, es geht dir gut.

I'm looking forward to hearing from you soon.	Ich freue mich darauf, bald von dir zu hören.

Let me know what you're doing.	Erzähl mir, was du machst.
Drop me a line!	
Please write soon.	} Schreib bald wieder!
Write (again) soon.	

Bye for now,	Tschüss!
See you (soon),	Bis bald,

Say hello to … for/from me.	Schöne Grüße an …
Give my regards/best wishes to…	Liebe Gruße an …
Take care!	Mach's gut!
All the best,	Alles Gute,
Yours,	Dein(e)
Kindest regards,	mit herzlichen Grüßen, herzlichst
Love (from),	liebe Grüße

(an Verwandte bzw. sehr gute Freunde)

⚠ Always start the first paragraph with a capital letter

4   Asking for information

Schloßstraße 6
D-74196 Bürg

Happy Days Riding School
attn. Mrs Hawtree
Dobson's Farm
Ashburton
Devon EX18 6PJ   19 May 1994

Dear Mrs Hawtree,

Last year my sister Britta spent a very interesting week at your riding school on Dartmoor.

This summer my English friend and I are planning to go on holiday in Devon and Cornwall. We are both interested in riding and would like to go pony trekking. Could you please send us some information about your school?

I will be staying with my English pen-friend in London for a week before we come to Devon. We are both 16 years old.

I look forward to hearing from you soon.
                            Yours sincerely,
                                        Karin Müller

5   Joining an association

25 Rillington Place
Gloucester GL3 6EP

Friends of the Earth
56-58 Alma Street
Luton
Beds. LU1 2YZ

25 February 1994

Dear Sir/Madam,

I read your magazine regularly in our school library. I am leaving school this summer, and would like to join Friends of the Earth.

If my GCSE results are good, I hope to go to Sixth Form College or Technical College in the autumn. So please enrol me as a student member.

I enclose a cheque from my mother for £8.

I very much look forward to hearing from you soon and to receiving my first 'personal' copy of your magazine.
                            Yours faithfully,
                                        Heather West

6   Useful phrases for a formal letter

attn. (= attention)
Dear Mr/Mrs/Miss Smith,
Dear Ms [mɪz] **Smith,**
(ehestandsunabhängig)
Dear Sir/Madam,
Sir,

z. Hd.
Lieber Herr/Liebe(s) Frau/Frl. Smith,
Liebe(s) Frau/Frl. Smith,

Sehr geehrte Damen und Herren,
Anrede in Leserbriefen an
Zeitungsredaktionen

I am writing for information
about ...
I am writing for further details
about ...

Ich möchte Sie bitten, mir
Informationen über ... zu schicken.
Ich möchte Sie bitten, mir Näheres
über ... zu senden.

Could you please send me ... ?

Würden Sie mir bitte ... zusenden?

I would like to join ...
Please enrol me as a member.

Ich möchte Mitglied von ... werden.
Bitte nehmen Sie mich als Mitglied
auf.

I enclose ...

Anbei finden Sie ...

I (very much) look forward to
hearing from you soon.

Ich freue mich (sehr) darauf, bald
von Ihnen zu hören.

Yours sincerely, [sɪnˈsɪəlɪ]
(In Briefen, die mit **Dear Mr/Mrs** *... usw., anfangen)*

mit freundlichen Grüßen

Yours faithfully, [ˈfeɪθfəlɪ]
(In Briefen, die mit **Dear Sir/Madam,** *anfangen)*

mit freundlichen Grüßen/Hoch-
achtungsvoll

⚠ Always use the postcode and put it at the end of the address.
⚠ Always start the first paragraph with a capital letter.

2   Saying what you think

Expressing an opinion

I think/don't think …	Ich glaube/glaube nicht …
I believe that …	Ich glaube, dass …
I find it strange that …	Ich finde es eigenartig, dass …
I'm sure that …	Ich bin mir sicher, dass …
In my opinion …	Meiner Meinung nach …
I suppose …	Ich nehme an, …
I think it's a good idea because …	Ich denke, es ist eine gute Idee, da …
It seems to me that …	Es scheint mir, dass …
I'm for/against the idea of…	Ich bin für/gegen die Idee …

Agreeing/disagreeing

I agree/disagree with you.	Ich teile deine/Ihre Meinung (nicht).
I think you're right/wrong.	Ich glaube du hast/Sie haben Recht/ unrecht.
That's quite true.	Das ist wahr.
That's not true at all.	Das ist überhaupt nicht wahr.
You can't really say that.	Das kann man eigentlich nicht sagen.
That's not the same.	Das ist nicht dasselbe.

Introducing a different argument

On the one hand … on the other (hand) …	Einerseits … andererseits …
They should either … or …	Sie sollten entweder … oder …
You have to look at the pros and cons.	Man muss das Für und Wider berücksichtigen.
We must consider the advantages and disavantages.	Wir müssen die Vor- und Nachteile in Betracht ziehen.
We must take the arguments on both sides into account.	Wir müssen die Argumente beider Seiten in Betracht ziehen.

⚠ Be careful!

I think …	Ich **meine** …
I mean …	Ich **will damit sagen** …
What does this word mean?	Was **heißt** dieses Wort?/ Was **bedeutet** dieses Wort?
Do you know the meaning of that word?	Kennst du die **Bedeutung** dieses Wortes?

3   False friends

1   Different meanings

actual ≠ aktuell

He actually knows the Queen.

This is a topical subject.

Er kennt die Königin **wirklich/ tatsächlich.**

Das ist ein **aktuelles** Thema.

also ≠ also

Her father also came.
So he did come after all.

Ihr Vater kam **auch.**
Er ist **also** doch gekommen.

bank

She works at a bank.

Sie arbeitet in einer **Bank.**
(Geldinstitut)

But **bank** ≠ **Bank** *in*
There is a new bench/seat
near the river bank.

Es gibt eine neue **Parkbank** am
Flussufer.

become ≠ bekommen

He became a pilot.
(become + noun = werden)
She became/got angry.
(get + adjective = werden)
I got a letter from her.
(get + noun = bekommen)

Er **wurde** Pilot.

Sie **wurde** wütend.

Ich **bekam** einen Brief von ihr.

---

*After waiting half an hour for his meal in a London restaurant,
a German tourist asked the waiter: "When will I become the steak
I ordered?" "Never, I hope, sir," was the waiter's shocked reply.*

---

blame ≠ blamieren
If you make a fool of yourself,
don't blame me!
Why do I always get the blame?

Wenn **du dich blamierst**, dann
gib mir bitte nicht die **Schuld!**
Warum bekomme immer ich die
Schuld?

brave ≠ brav

It was brave of her to jump into the river to save the dog.
Be good!

Es war **mutig** von ihr, in den Fluss zu springen, um den Hund zu retten.
Sei brav!

chips ≠ Chips

Fish and chips
(potato) crisps

Fisch und **Pommes frites**
Kartoffelchips

critic ≠ Kritik

The film critic of *The Times* wrote a long review of the film.

Der **Filmkritiker** der *Times* schrieb eine lange **Kritik** über den Film.

Meaning ≠ Meinung

Do you know the meaning of that word?
In my opinion …

Kennst du die **Bedeutung** dieses Wortes?
Meiner **Meinung** nach …

note ≠ Note

I'll make a note of it.
Did you get my note?
What mark did you get?

Have you got your music?

Ich **schreib's auf.**
Hast du meinen **Zettel** bekommen?
Was für eine **Note** hast du bekommen?
Hast du deine **Noten**?

photograph ≠ Fotograf/in

My sister is a photographer.
Have you seen her photographs?

Meine Schwester ist **Fotografin.**
Hast du ihre **Fotos** gesehen?

recipe ≠ (ärztliches) Rezept

The doctor gave him a prescription.
but:
Have you got a recipe for …?

Die Ärztin gab ihm ein **Rezept.**

Hast du ein (Koch-)**Rezept** für …?

sensible ≠ sensibel

It was a sensible decision.	Es war eine **vernünftige** Entscheidung.
He's a sensitive boy.	Er ist ein **sensibler** Junge.

small ≠ schmal

It is a small town with narrow streets.	Es ist eine **kleine** Stadt/**Klein**stadt mit **schmalen** Straßen.
She's got a thin face.	Sie hat ein **schmales** Gesicht.

spend ≠ spenden

I spent a lot of money at the weekend.	Ich **habe** sehr viel Geld am Wochenende **ausgegeben.**
They donated £50 to the Red Cross.	Sie **spendeten** dem Roten Kreuz £ 50.
We spent two weeks in Italy.	Wir **haben** zwei Wochen in Italien **verbracht.**

sympathetic ≠ sympathisch

He was very sympathetic when he heard the story.	Er **zeigte** sehr viel **Mitgefühl,** als er die Geschichte hörte.
I like her parents a lot. I think her parents are very nice.	Ihre Eltern sind mir sehr **sympathisch.**

2   Different spellings in British English

address	Adresse	**litre**	Liter
career	Karriere	**model**	Modell
carnival	Karneval	**per cent**	Prozent
catalogue	Katalog	**photo**	Foto
colleague	Kollege	**rhyme**	Reim
kilometre	Kilometer	**second**	Sekunde
licence	Lizenz	**wonder**	Wunder

⚠ German words ending in "er" like *Meter* and *Liter* are spelt the same in American English (meter, liter).

4   Singular and plural words

1   True and false pairs

'True' pairs are always **two** things: a pair of shoes = **two** shoes.
The noun can be used in the singular or plural with a singular or plural verb:
e.g. My left shoe **is** gone! Both shoes **were** in the kitchen yesterday.

Some pairs are 'false' pairs. They are used for **one** thing:
a pair of jeans = **one** piece of clothing with two legs.
With false pairs there is no singular form of the noun, and you need a plural verb:
e.g. My trousers **are** too small.
If you want to use 'a/an' or a number with false pairs you must use the words 'pair(s) of':
e.g. She had two **pairs of** glasses.

True pairs – two objects

one glove/two gloves	ein Handschuh/zwei Handschuhe
a pair of shoes/socks/gloves/ rollerskates/ice-skates	ein Paar Schuhe/Socken/Hand- schuhe/Roll-/Schlittschuhe

False pairs – one object

(a pair of) **trousers** (*AE* pants)	(eine) Hose
(a pair of) **jeans**	(eine) Jeans-Hose
(a pair of) **shorts**	(eine) kurze Hose
(a pair of) **pyjamas** (*AE* pajamas)	(ein) Schlafanzug
(a pair of) **tights**	(eine) Strumpfhose
(a pair of) **scissors**	(eine) Schere
(a pair of) **glasses**	(eine) Brille
(a pair of) **binoculars**	(ein) Fernglas

2   Other plural nouns which are singular in German

scales	Waage
stairs	Treppe
handlebars	Lenkstange
clothes	Kleidung

3   No plural in English – plural in German

The nouns 'information', 'advice', 'news' 'homework' and 'furniture'
are only used as collectives (like 'milk', 'bread') in English, although
they have a plural in German. If you use them with 'a/an' or a number,
you need words like 'a piece of/a bit of', 'two pieces of':

The information was interesting. It was an interesting piece of information.	Die **Information(en)** war(en) interessant. Es war eine interessante **Information.**
He gave me several pieces of advice. I thanked him for his advice. Let me give you a bit of advice.	Er gab mir mehrere **Ratschläge.** Ich dankte ihm für seinen **Rat.** Darf ich Ihnen **einen Rat** geben?
The news is good. That's an interesting piece of news.	Die **Nachrichten** sind gut. Das ist eine interessante **Neuigkeit.**
Is homework really necessary?	Sind **Hausaufgaben** wirklich nötig?
I like your furniture! I bought several new pieces of furniture last week.	Eure **Möbel** gefallen mir. Ich kaufte letzte Woche mehrere neue **Möbel(stücke).**

4   Plural noun, singular verb

The USA is a big country.		Die **USA sind** ein großes Land.	
Maths Physics Gymnastics	**is** my favourite subject.	**Mathematik Physik Gymnastik**	**ist** mein Lieblingsfach.

5   Singular noun, plural verb

We use a plural verb with grammatically 'singular' nouns that refer to
a group of people:

The police were waiting for him.	Die **Polizei wartete** auf ihn.
The crowd are on their feet as the athletes come into the stadium.	Das ganze **Stadion ist auf den Beinen,** als die Athleten hereinkommen.

5   Describing what people are like

1   Describing what people look like

blond(e) **fair-haired**	} blond
dark-haired	dunkelhaarig
bald	kahl
pretty	hübsch
beautiful	schön
good-looking	gut aussehend
ugly [ʌ]	hässlich
small, short	klein
tall	groß
curly-haired	mit lockigen Haaren
straight-haired	mit glatten Haaren
slim	schlank
well-built	stämmig
thin	dünn
fat	dick
moustache [məˈstɑːʃ]	Schnurrbart
beard	Bart
well-dressed	gut angezogen

2 Describing character and qualities

careful	vorsichtig	**careless**	nachlässig
clever/smart	klug	**stupid**	dumm, blöd
friendly	freundlich	**unfriendly**	unfreundlich
generous ['dʒenərəs]	großzügig	**greedy**	gierig
helpful	hilfsbereit	**unhelpful**	unhilfsbereit
honest ['ɒnɪst]	ehrlich	**dishonest**	unehrlich
interesting	interessant	**boring**	langweilig
kind	nett, freundlich	**cruel** ['kruəl]	grausam
hard-working	fleißig	**lazy**	faul
modest	bescheiden	**proud**	stolz
nice	nett	**nasty**	gemein
optimistic [‚--'--]	optimistisch	**pessimistic** [‚--'--]	pessimistisch
patient ['peɪʃnt]	geduldig	**impatient**	ungeduldig
polite	höflich	**impolite/rude**	unhöflich
positive	positiv	**negative**	negativ
quiet	ruhig	**loud/noisy**	laut
relaxed	entspannt	**tense**	gespannt
selfish	egoistisch	**unselfish**	uneigennützig
sensible ['---]	vernünftig	**silly**	albern
serious	ernst	**light-hearted**	unbekümmert
shy	schüchtern	**out-going**	extravertiert
strong	stark	**weak**	schwach
thoughtful	nachdenklich	**thoughtless**	gedankenlos

3 Describing how people feel

angry	wütend/zornig
bored	gelangweilt
confident	selbstsicher
depressed	niedergeschlagen
disappointed	enttäuscht
excited	aufgeregt
happy	froh, glücklich
lonely	einsam
nervous ['--]	nervös
pleased	erfreut, zufrieden
surprised	überrascht
tired	müde
unhappy/sad	traurig
worried	besorgt

– *I have six legs, two bodies, fifteen eyes, four noses and forty fingers on each hand. What am I?*
– *Ugly.*

6   Spelling and pronounciation

1.   Some words pronounced the same but spelt differently:

Peter: John! Sam! Sheila! Where is everybody?

John: Hello, Peter. What's up?

Peter: Oh, here you are, John. Why don't the others hear me calling?

John: I'm sure they all went down to the sea a few minutes ago.
Do you need some help?

Peter: Would you fetch some wood for the fire?

John: But I promised Sheila I'd meet her at the supermarket and help
her to buy the meat for the barbecue. Can't you ask someone
else?

Peter: Who? Sam's sitting in the sun playing with his son. The others
have gone to see the sea. I expect they're sitting down there
with their feet in the water while I do all the work!

John: Poor Peter! Never mind! Shall I pour you a cup of tea before I get
the food?

[hɪə] = here, hear   [wʊd] = would, wood   [miːt] = meet, meat
[sʌn] = sun, son   [siː] = see, sea   [ðeə] = there, their
[pɔː] = poor, pour

Two robbers too many – watch your spelling!

Two men wanted to rob a bank when it opened at two o'clock. But they
were too late. Two other men had had the same idea, too. These two
men hid in the bank just before the people in the bank went to lunch.
Then they started to break into the safe. But they were too slow. When
the manager returned at exactly two minutes to two, he saw the other
two men waiting outside the bank. So he went to the police station to
get help. When they saw the police coming, the two men outside the
bank ran off. The men inside the bank wanted to escape, too, but the
police were too quick for them. They were arrested and taken to the
police station.

The robbers did not know that there was no money in the safe. It was
an old safe, and the bank manager knew that a new safe would be
delivered that afternoon, so the old safe was empty.

[nəʊ] = no, know   [njuː] = new, knew   [tuː] = two, too

[blu:]

A strong wind blew the blue car off the road.

Ein starker Wind stieß das blaue Auto von der Straße.

[θru:]

The new boy threw a stone through the school window.

Der Neue warf einen Stein durchs Fenster.

[wi:k], ['auə]

Manchester United has had a weak week:
"But our hour will come!" said the manager.

Manchester United hatte eine schwache Woche:
"Unsere Stunde wird aber kommen!" sagte der Manager.

[raɪt]

Write the right answer on a postcard and send it to Mr Wright.

Schreiben Sie die richtige Antwort auf eine Postkarte, und schicken Sie sie an Mr Wright.

2   Same spelling, different pronunciation

row

They were sitting in the front row [rəʊ].
He had a row [raʊ] with his wife.

Sie saßen in der ersten Reihe.
Er hatte Krach mit seiner Frau.

bow

A bow [bəʊ] and arrow.
Robin Hood bowed [baʊd] to the Sheriff.

Ein Pfeil und Bogen.
Robin Hood verbeugte sich vor dem Sheriff.

live

We live [liv] in Britain.
There was live [laɪv] music at the party.

Wir leben in Großbritannien.
Es gab Live-Musik bei der Party.

"What is black and white and red all over?"
"I don't know! How can something be black, white and red all over?"
"Well, a newspaper is printed in black and white – but it's re(a)d, too!"

7   Make or do?

What shall we do?

Jane: It's a wonderful day today. What shall we do this afternoon?

Pete: Let's go for a cycle ride in the country! We haven't done that for a long time.

Matt: But I've got to do some German homework. We've got a test tomorrow.

Jane: Can't you do that when we come back, Matt?

Matt: OK. Shall we make some sandwiches?

Jane: Good idea. You can do that. And I'll take my camera so I can take a few pictures for our photographic activity at school.

Pete: Can you make some tea to take with us, too?

Matt: Can't you do your share of the work and make the tea?

Jane: Do stop arguing you two, or we'll never get everything done.

In English, the verb 'make' often means *machen* in the sense of 'to actually produce', 'to construct', 'to build". The verb 'do' often means *tun/machen* in the sense of the German verb *erledigen:*

She made a model plane.	Sie **baute** ein Modellflugzeug.
He did his homework.	Er **machte** *(= löste)* seine Schulaufgaben.
We did the test.	Wir **machten** *(= schrieben)* den Test.

to make = machen

She made the beds.	Sie **machte die Betten.**
Anyone can make a mistake.	Jeder kann **einen Fehler machen.**
Don't make so much noise!	**Macht nicht soviel Krach!**
We made a mess in the kitchen.	Wir **machten viel Unordnung** in der Küche.
She made fun of me.	Sie **machte sich lustig über mich.**
It is made of wood.	Es ist **aus** Holz (gemacht).

to do = machen

What did I do wrong?	Was habe ich (da) **falsch gemacht?**
What do you do for a living?	Was **machen Sie beruflich?**
I've got to do my homework.	Ich muss **meine Hausaufgaben machen.**
He does his share of the work.	Er **macht seinen Anteil der Arbeit.**

to do = tun

I've got nothing to do today.	Heute habe ich nichts zu **tun.**
What can I do for you?	**Was kann ich für dich/Sie tun?**
You could do me a big favour.	Du könntest mir **einen großen Gefallen tun.**

⚠ **machen ≠ to make**

We went for a cycle ride.	Wir **machten eine Radtour.**
I took a photo.	Ich **machte ein Foto.**

⚠ **to make/to do = different constructions in English and German**

He made friends with her.	Er hat **sich mit ihr angefreundet.**
Make up your mind.	**Entscheide dich doch!**
They made me wait.	Sie **ließen** mich warten.
He made that story up.	Die Geschichte hat er **erfunden.**
He made his fortune in America.	Er **wurde** in Amerika **reich.**
Make sure the windows are closed before you leave.	**Sorge dafür,** dass alle Fenster zu sind, bevor du gehst.
Can you make the tea?	Kannst du **den Tee kochen?**
I make a lot of cakes.	Ich **backe viel.**

That will do!	**Das reicht!/Das genügt!**
I've done the shopping.	Ich **habe eingekauft.**
She did well in her exams.	Sie **schnitt in der Prüfung gut ab.**
He does a paper round.	Er **trägt Zeitungen aus.**
If there is not enough food, some people will have to do without.	Wenn es nicht genug zu essen gibt, müssen eben einige **ohne auskommen/ darauf verzichten.**
Do you think we'll be able to do it all?	Glaubst du, das alles werden wir **schaffen können?**
We'll never get it all done.	Wir werden das alles nie **schaffen.**

to make do

We'll just have to make do with what we've got.	Wir werden einfach mit dem, was wir haben, **auskommen** müssen.

8   Useful expressions with common verbs

to be ...

less formal	**more formal**	
He is in.	He **is at home.**	zu Hause sein
He is out.	He **is not at home.**	nicht zu Hause sein
She is away in Scotland.	She **has gone** to Scotland.	verreist sein
It's difficult. Are you up to it?	It's difficult. **Can** you **do it**?	der Sache gewachsen sein
You're up early!	You have **got up** early!	früh auf sein
We're off now!	We**'re leaving** now!	losfahren
The milk is off.	The milk **has turned bad.**	schlecht geworden sein
The match is off.	The match **has been cancelled.**	abgesagt werden
The race is on today.	The race **takes place** today.	stattfinden
They'll be back this evening.	They'll **return** this evening.	zurückkommen
The programme is over.	The programme **has finished.**	vorbei sein
What are the kids up to?	What **are** the children **doing**?	heimlich tun, anstellen
I'm for doing the washing-up first.	I **think it would be a good idea** to do the washing-up first.	Ich bin dafür, dass ….
I'm against waiting for them.	I **don't think it would be a good idea** to wait for them.	Ich bin dagegen, dass …

to bring ...

Our new boss has brought about many changes.	etwas herbeiführen
Bring a couple of friends along.	mitbringen
Both her parents died, so her aunt brought her up.	großziehen, aufziehen
I'm glad you brought that point up.	etwas erwähnen/ins Spiel bringen

to come ...

After a few days the handle came off.	sich lösen
Come on! We're late already.	Los! Gehen wir!
What did you do yesterday evening?	
Peter came round and we watched a film.	vorbeischauen,-kommen
My dream has come true.	wahr werden

to get ...

She got dressed immediately.	sich anziehen
She got up at 6.15.	aufstehen
The train got in at midnight.	ankommen
I got on the bus at the station and	einsteigen
got off at the airport.	aussteigen
We hope you get better soon.	gesund werden
Get well soon!	Gute Besserung!
Sorry I'm late – I got lost.	sich verlaufen, verfahren
The talk was not very interesting, so we soon got bored.	sich langweilen
She doesn't get on with her mother.	mit jdm auskommen
The prisoners got away.	entkommen
He got away with the robbery.	ungestraft davonkommen
How are you getting on with your work?	mit etwas weiter-, vorankommen
Mum got to know Dad in Bristol.	kennen lernen
I soon got used to working outdoors.	sich an etwas gewöhnen
He still hasn't got over his grandmother's death.	über etwas hinwegkommen
The weather is getting me down.	... macht mich ganz fertig
Hurry up and get ready! We're late.	sich fertig machen
Haven't you got rid of that cough?	etwas loswerden

to go ...

Let's go for a walk.	spazieren gehen
"Go on," said the policeman.	Erzählen Sie weiter!
Why is there so much noise? What's going on here?	Was ist hier los?/Was geht hier vor?
Mum nearly went mad when she heard.	verrückt werden

The workers are going on strike next week.   streiken
The bomb went off at 7 a.m.   explodieren
Is the lesson over already? It went by   vorbeigehen
really quickly today.

to have ...

I had a shower after the match.   (sich) duschen
We had breakfast in the kitchen.   frühstücken
They always have tea at six o'clock.   Abendbrot essen
I often have a cold in the winter.   erkältet sein
She had her car repaired last week.   reparieren lassen
They have little in common.   gemeinsam haben
I've got to leave at six so that I don't miss   müssen
my train.

to keep ...

I try to keep fit.   fit bleiben
Danger! Keep out!   Eintritt verboten!
He kept on trying.   immer wieder versuchen
Keep to the footpaths.   Bleiben Sie auf den
    Fußwegen.
Keep to the rules!   sich an etwas halten

to look ...

Look at this picture.   (sich) etwas anschauen
He looked up and saw her.   aufblicken
Look up their number in the   nachschlagen
telephone book.
The police are looking into his alibi.   untersuchen/überprüfen
She's looking for a better job.   nach etwas suchen
I'm looking forward to my holiday.   sich freuen auf
Look out!   Pass auf!

When the sailor on the English cross-channel ferry wanted to throw a bucket of dirty water into the sea, he shouted "Look out!" to warn passengers on the lower deck. He did not expect three Frenchmen on the lower deck to look out of one of the windows!

Look after the baby while I do the shopping. — auf jdn aufpassen

She looks down on everybody. — verachten

He looks up to his teacher. — respektieren

Look in on your way home. — hereinschauen

He looks like his brother. — aussehen (wie)

to put …

He put down his book. — hinlegen

The army put the rebellion down. — niederschlagen

Put that down in your notebook. — aufschreiben

They soon put out the fire. — löschen

Take off your coat and put a pullover on. — anziehen

If you don't like it, you'll have to put up with it. — mit etwas leben, sich mit etwas abfinden

If Mr Smith phones, put him through. — durchstellen

She's put her name down for tennis lessons. — sich für etwas eintragen

He was put out that he wasn't invited. — verärgert sein

Can we put off our meeting till next week? — verschieben

to run …

He runs a hotel on the edge of town. — führen, betreiben

The trains do not run in the winter. — verkehren, fahren

The children ran away. — weglaufen

My walkman isn't working. The batteries have run down. — schwach/leer werden

He nearly ran over a cat on his way to work. — überfahren

We ran out of petrol last week. — … ging uns aus

You run the risk of losing your licence. — Gefahr laufen

She ran up to me. — auf jdn zulaufen

to take …

I took him for his brother. — jdn für jdn anders halten

Our plane took off ten minutes late. — starten

They took off their shoes. — ausziehen

He has taken up skiing as a hobby. — aufnehmen, anfangen mit

She takes after her mother. — ähnlich sehen

The referee took out his whistle. — zücken, hervorholen

We took a few photos/pictures. — Fotos machen

The doctor took my temperature.	Temperatur/Fieber messen
The policewoman took our names and addresses.	aufschreiben
The competition takes place next week.	stattfinden
Do you still want to take part?	teilnehmen
I often take the dog for a walk.	spazieren gehen mit
I took hold of his hand.	
I took him by the hand.	jdn bei der Hand fassen
We must take a chance.	etwas riskieren
Can't we take turns?	sich abwechseln
We took a wrong turning in Leeds.	falsch abbiegen
I took it apart/to pieces.	auseinander nehmen
My brother has taken over my parents' restaurant.	übernehmen
The firm is taking on three new employees.	einstellen
Take care!	Mach's gut!
I'm feeling tired. Shall we take a break?	eine Pause machen
He's taking an English course.	einen Kurs machen

to turn ...

Turn that TV off and turn the radio on.	ausschalten/einschalten
Turn up the volume – I can't hear what they're saying.	hochdrehen, lauter machen
He was offered the job but he turned it down.	ablehnen
Is it my turn now?	dran/an der Reihe sein
Miss a turn.	(eine Runde) aussetzen
The ugly prince turned into a beautiful frog.	sich in etwas verwandeln

9   Problem words in German

beide, einer von beiden

Beide trugen schwarze Sachen.	They **both** wore black.
Beide waren bewaffnet.	They were **both** armed.
Die Polizei sucht nach den beiden Macbraynes.	The police are looking for **the two** Macbraynes.
Es gibt eine $ 100 Belohnung für die Festnahme von einem der beiden.	$100 reward for the capture of **either of them.**
Beide Züge halten in Bath. Sie können beide nehmen.	**Both** trains stop at Bath. You can take **either of them.**

bringen

Du kannst einen Freund mitbringen.	You can **bring** a friend along.
Kannst du mir eine Zeitschrift (her)bringen?	Can you **bring** me a magazine?
Könntest du mich zum Bahnhof (hin)bringen.	Could you **take** me to the station?

fahren, gehen

Ich gehe jede Woche ins Kino.	I **go** to the cinema every week.
Ich fahre manchmal mit dem Bus.	I sometimes **go by bus.**
Der nächste Bus fährt um sechs.	The next bus **leaves** at six.
Meine Mutter fährt mit dem Auto zur Arbeit.	My mother **drives** to work.
Ich fahre mit dem Rad in die Schule, aber er geht zu Fuß hin.	I **cycle** to school but he **walks.**
Wir fahren oft mit der Bahn.	We often **take the/go by** train.

sagen

Er sagte "Guten Tag". *(with direct speech)*	He **said** "Good morning".
Er sagte, er wohne in London. *(with indirect statement)*	He **said** he lived in London.
Sag mir, wo du wohnst.	**Tell me** where you live.

so

Sie spielt nicht **so** gut.	She doesn't play **so** well.
Er spielt nicht **so** gut wie ich.	He doesn't play **as** well as I do.
Er ist **so** lieb.	He's **so** nice.
So ein Unsinn!	**What** nonsense!
Er hat **so** einen lieben Hund.	He's got **such** a nice dog.

spielen, Spiel

Wir **spielen** jeden Tag Fußball.	We **play** football every day.
Er **spielt** Schlagzeug.	He **plays** the drums.
Sie **spielte** Julia in unserer Schulaufführung.	She **played** Juliet in our school play.
Alle Schauspieler **spielten** Ihre Rollen sehr gut.	All the actors **played/acted** their parts very well.
Im **Spiel** am Samstag **spielte** die Mannschaft sehr gut.	The team **played** very well in Saturday's **match/game.**
Es spielt keine Rolle.	**It makes no difference.**

Stück

ein **Stück** Kuchen	a **piece** of cake
ein **(Musik-)Stück** von Mozart	a **piece of music** by Mozart
ein **(Theater-)Stück** von Goethe	a **play** by Goethe

A young English student rushed into a small German post office just before closing time one evening. He wanted to weigh a parcel but was in such a hurry that he mixed up his German vowels. He smiled at the young girl behind the counter and said:
"Haben Sie eine Wiege? Ich will etwas wagen!"

10   One word in German, two or more in English

alle/Alles

Alle Kühe essen Gras.	**All** cows eat grass.
Alle Kühe in diesem Feld gehören Herrn Smith.	**All the** cows in this field belong to Mr Smith.
alle zwei Jahre	**every** two years
Haben wir alles?	Have we got **everything?**
Sind alle da?	Is **everyone** there?

als

Als ich ihn sah, winkte er.	**When** I saw him he waved.
Er sah älter aus als auf dem Bild.	He looked older **than** on the photo.
Gerade als ich ankam, fuhr der Bus los.	Just **as** I arrived the bus drove off.
Er verkleidete sich als Frau.	He dressed up **as** a woman.

bei

The German preposition 'bei' is only rarely translated by the English word 'by':

Bei Tag, Nacht	**By** day/night
Sie nahm mich bei der Hand.	She took me **by** the hand.
But:	
Wir wohnten bei Freunden.	We stayed **with** friends.
Gestern war ich bei meiner Tante.	I was **at** my aunt's yesterday.
Ich wohne in Watford bei London.	I live in Watford, **near** London.
Sie arbeitet bei Rolls Royce.	She works **at/for** Rolls Royce.
Jetzt ist er beim Militär.	He's **in the army** now.
Beim Lesen des Artikels ...	**When reading** the article, ...

besuchen

Er besucht sie jede Woche.	He **visits** her every week.
Sie besucht eine Privatschule.	She **goes to/attends** a private school.

bis

Wir müssen bis 16.00 Uhr in der Schule bleiben.	We have to stay at school **until** 4 o'clock. *(until = length of action)*
Er muss bis (spätestens) halb zehn am Bahnhof sein – sein Zug fährt um 9.45 Uhr.	He has to be at the station **by** half past nine – his train leaves at 9.45. *(by = before)*

Bus

Wir nahmen den Bus zum
Bahnhof. *(Bus = Linienbus, meist im Stadtverkehr)*
Der (Reise)bus war sehr bequem.
(Bus = Reisebus, Überlandbus)

We took the **bus** to the station.

The **coach** was very comfortable.

erinnern

Sie erinnert mich an ihren Bruder. She **reminds** me of her brother.
Ich muss Susi morgen anrufen. I've got to phone Susi tomorrow.
Kannst du mich daran erinnern? Can you **remind me** about it/to do
it?

Wir waren vor zehn Jahren hier. We were here ten years ago. Do you
Erinnerst du dich daran? **remember (it)**?

fertig

Bist du fertig? *(Kann's losgehen?)*   Are you **ready**?
Bist du fertig? *(am Ende einer Arbeit)* Have you **finished**?
Als ich ankam, war ich fix und I was **exhausted/tired out** when I
fertig! arrived.

Geschichte

Er erzählte mir eine Geschichte.   He told me a **story.**
Geschichte ist mein Lieblingsfach. **History** is my favourite subject.

glücklich, Glück

Ich hatte sehr viel Glück. I was very **lucky.**
Was für ein Glück! **What luck!**
Er war glücklich, sie zu sehen. He was **happy** to see her.
Glück kann man nicht kaufen. Money doesn't buy **happiness.**

groß

Napoleon war kein großer Mann, Napoleon was not a **big/tall** man
aber ein großer General. but he was a **great** general.

hoch

Snowdon ist ein hoher Berg. Snowdon is a **high** mountain.
Sie starb im hohen Alter. She died at a **great** age.

hören

Wir **hörten** die Explosion.	We **heard** the explosion.
Wir **hörten** die Sendung.	We **listened to** the broadcast.
Er **hatte nie von** Einstein **gehört**.	He **had never heard of** Einstein.

jeder

Wir gehen **jeden** Tag dorthin.	We go there **every/each** day.
Das weiß **jeder**.	**Everyone** knows that.
Das weiß **jeder** Dummkopf!	**Any fool** knows that!
	(any = jeder x-beliebige)
Er gab **jedem von uns** einen Apfel.	He gave **each of us** an apple.

Land

Großbritannien ist kein riesiges **Land**.	Britain is not a huge **country**.
Wir wohnen **auf dem Land**.	We live **in the country**.
Er besitzt viel **Land**.	He owns a lot of **land**.
Leute **aus allen Ländern**.	People **from all over the world**.

lassen

	"let" + infinitive without "to"
Er **lässt mich** manchmal **fahren**. *(erlauben)*	He sometimes **lets me drive**.
Die Polizei **ließ sie laufen**.	The police **let them go**.
Ich **ließ** das Buch **fallen**.	I **dropped** the book.
Ich **ließ** das Buch auf dem Tisch (liegen).	I **left** the book on the table.
	"have" + object + past participle
Er **ließ** sein Auto **reparieren**.	He **had** his car **repaired**.

nächste(r/s)

Wo ist die **nächste** Haltestelle? Wir müssen mit dem **nächsten** Bus fahren.	Where is the **nearest** *(closest)* bus stop? We have to get the **next** *(in sequence)* bus.

noch/noch nicht

Es gibt **noch viel** zu tun.	There is **still a lot** to do.
Hast du den Film **noch nicht** gesehen?	Have**n't** you seen that film **yet**?

Gib' mir noch etwas Milch, bitte.	Please give me **a little more** milk.
Sie hat immer noch einen Brief zu schreiben.	She **still** has one more letter to write.
Sind noch Plätze frei?	Are there **(still)** any seats left?

ein paar, Paar

Ich borgte mir ein paar Pfund, um mir ein Paar Handschuhe zu kaufen.	I borrowed **a couple of** pounds to buy myself **a pair of** gloves.
Sie und ihr Freund sind ein glückliches Paar.	She and her boyfriend make a happy **couple.**

Preis

Der neue Preis beträgt £ 10.	The new **price** [praɪs] is £10.
Er gewann den ersten Preis im Wettbewerb.	He won first **prize** [praɪz] in the competition.

schon

Ich habe meine Hausaufgaben schon gemacht.	I've **already** done my homework.
Schon früh konnte er Klavier spielen.	He was able to play the piano **at an early age.**
Schon damals haben alle Leute sein Klavierspiel bewundert.	**Even then** everyone admired the way he played the piano.
Ich warte schon seit sechs Monaten.	I've been waiting for six months **(now)**.

'schon' is often left untranslated in sentences like:

Ich komme (ja) schon!	I'm coming!
Sie wohnen schon seit Jahren hier.	They've been living here for years.

schwer

Der Koffer war zu schwer.	The suitcase was too **heavy.**
Das Problem war sehr schwer zu lösen.	The problem was very **difficult** to solve.

seit

Er ist seit Wochen krank.	He has been ill **for weeks.** *(for + period of time)*
Er ist seit 14. Mai in Urlaub.	He has been on holiday **since 14th May.** *(since + point in time)*

sehen

Ich **habe** dich gestern in der Stadt **gesehen**.
I **saw** you in town yesterday.

Wir **haben** den Film im Fernsehen **gesehen**.
We **saw/watched** the film on TV.

Sie **sieht** fern.
She is **watching TV.**

Sie **sahen** sich die Unterschrift genau **an**.
They **looked at** the signature carefully.

Sie **sah** gesund **aus**.
She **looked** well. *(adjective!)*

Stock

Sie hatte einen Unfall und geht nun am **Stock**.
She had an accident and now walks with a **stick.**

Sie wohnt im dritten **Stock**.
She lives on the third **floor.**

Ich wohne in einem **drei-stöckigen** Haus.
I live in a **three storey** house/a house with **three floors.**

viel

Hast du **viel** Gepäck mitgebracht?
Did you bring **much** luggage with you? *(much + singular noun)*

Hast du **viele** Taschen?
Have you got **many** bags? *(many + plural noun)*

vor

Sie war nervös **vor** der Prüfung.
She was nervous **before** the exam. *(time)*

Er stand **vor** ihr.
He stood **in front of** her. *(place)*

während

Er ist **während** des Films eingeschlafen.
He fell asleep **during** the film. *(during + noun)*

Während wir nach Hause fuhren, hatten wir einen Unfall.
While we were on our way home, we had an accident. *(while + verb)*

tragen

Sie **trug** ein neues Kleid.
She **was wearing** a new dress.

Sie **trug** auch eine Handtasche.
She also **carried** a handbag.

Uhr

Abends nehme ich immer meine **(Armband-)Uhr** ab.
I always take my **watch** off at night.

Eine große Uhr hängt an der Wand.	There's a large **clock** on the wall.
Wieviel Uhr ist es?	**What time** is it?

wenn

Ich sag's ihm, wenn ich ihn sehen sollte. *(falls)*	I'll tell him **if** I see him.
Ich sag's ihm, wenn ich ihn heute Nachmittag sehe.	I'll tell him **when** I see him this afternoon.

(zu irgendeinem Zeitpunkt in der Zukunft)

Auch wenn er noch recht jung ist, weiß er eine Menge.	**Even though** he's still quite young he knows a lot.
Immer wenn ich ihr schreibe, grüße ich sie von dir.	**Whenever** I write to her I send her your best wishes

werden

Es wird dunkel.	It's **getting** dark.
Es wurde bald kühler.	The weather soon **turned** colder.
Sie wird schnell wütend.	She quickly **gets** angry.
Er wurde Polizist.	He **became** a policeman.
Er wurde rot.	He **went red.**/He **blushed.**

wie

Wie machst du das?	**How** do you do that?
Wie bitte?	**Sorry?/Pardon?**
Wie bitte? (= Was?)	**What?**
Wie war das mit dem Auto?	**What** was that about the car?
Er lebt wie Gott in Frankreich.	He lives **like** a king.
Wie du weißt, ist er schon weg.	**As you know**, he has already left.
Sie ist so klug wie ihre Mutter.	She is **as** clever **as** her mother.

zuerst

(Zu)erst biegen Sie links ab, dann fahren Sie geradeaus bis zur nächsten Ampel.	**First** turn left, then drive straight on to the next traffic lights.

(erstens ... zweitens ... drittens)

Zuerst war ich etwas erstaunt.	**At first** I was rather surprised.

(anfänglich)

11   One word in English, two or more in German

before

Be home before eleven.	Sei **vor** elf zu Hause.
Say goodbye before you go.	Sag' auf Wiedersehen, **bevor** du gehst.

fair

That's not fair!	Das ist nicht **fair**!
We went to the fair.	Wir gingen zum **Jahrmarkt.**
He's got fair hair.	Er hat **blonde** Haare.

fault

Why blame me? It's not my fault.	Warum gibst du mir die Schuld? Es ist nicht meine **Schuld.**
He has many faults.	Er hat viele **Fehler.**

get *(see page* 133*)*

kind

That was kind of you.	Das war **nett** von dir.
What kind of car have they got?	**Was für** ein Auto haben sie?
I don't like these biscuits. Have you got any other kind?	Ich mag diese Kekse nicht. Haben Sie eine andere **Sorte**?

know

I know him by sight, but I don't know his name.	Ich **kenne** ihn vom Sehen, aber ich **weiß** seinen Namen nicht.
Mum got to know Dad in Bristol.	Mutti **lernte** Vati in Bristol **kennen.**

like

He looks like his father.	Er **sieht aus wie** sein Vater.
They like their mother.	Sie **mögen** ihre Mutter.
What's the weather like today?	**Wie** ist das Wetter heute?

own

He owns a car.	Er **besitzt** ein Auto.
He has a car of his own.	Er hat ein **eigenes** Auto.

place

Edinburgh is an interesting place.	Edinburgh ist ein interessanter **Ort.**
Pick me up at my place.	Hol' mich von **meiner Wohnung** ab.
We'll meet at my place.	Wir treffen uns **bei mir.**
The race takes place every year.	Das Rennen **findet** jedes Jahr **statt.**
He finished in third place.	Er belegte den dritten **Platz.**
He came third.	

"Let's enjoy it while we can – this is the place where they're going to build the new leisure centre."

pretty

Sue is very pretty.	Sue ist sehr **hübsch.**
Sue was pretty angry with me.	Sue war **ziemlich** böse auf mich.

rest

Have a rest!	**Ruh' dich aus!**
The rest of the week is free.	Der **Rest der Woche** ist frei.
The rest of us stayed at home.	Die **Übrigen** blieben zu Hause.

run *(also see page 135)*

She **ran** to the bus stop.	Sie **lief** zur Bushaltestelle.
He **ran into** a tree last week.	Letzte Woche **fuhr er gegen** einen Baum.
I **ran into** him yesterday.	Ich **traf** ihn **(zufällig)** gestern.

take *(see pages 135-6)*

trip

We went on a **day trip** to London.	Wir machten einen **Tagesausflug** nach London.
When I **tripped over** a stone my friend said, "**Have a nice trip!**"	Als ich **über** einen Stein **stolperte,** sagte mein Bekannter "**Gute Reise!**"

use

I always **use** the Underground when I'm in London.	Wenn ich in London bin, **benutze** ich immer die U-Bahn.
I **used** [ju:zd] your phone last night.	Gestern Abend **habe** ich dein Telefon **benutzt.**
We **used** [ju:st] **to** live in Germany.	Wir **wohnten früher** in Deutschland.
We are **used** [ju:st] **to** speaking German.	Wir sind es **gewohnt,** Deutsch zu sprechen.
We soon got **used** [ju:st] **to** eating German food.	Wir **gewöhnten** uns bald **ans** deutsche Essen.

Irregular Verbs

	Past tense	Past participle
to be	was	been
to beat	beat	beaten
to blow	blew	blown [əʊ]
to break	broke	broken
to bring	brought	brought
to broadcast	broadcast/broadcasted	broadcast/broadcasted
to build	built	built
to burn	burnt/burned	burnt/burned
to catch	caught	caught
to choose	chose	chosen
to come	came	come
to cost	cost	cost
to cut	cut	cut
to do	did	done
to draw	drew	drawn
to dream	dreamt/dreamed	dreamt/dreamed
to drink	drank	drunk
to drive	drove	driven
to fall	fell	fallen
to fight	fought	fought
to flee	fled	fled
to fly	flew	flown
to freeze	froze	frozen
to get	got	got
to give	gave	given
to go	went	gone
to grow	grew	grown
to hang = *(auf)hängen*	hung	hung
= *(er)hängen*	hanged	hanged
to have	had	had
to keep	kept	kept
to know	knew	known

	Past tense	Past participle
to lead	led	led
to learn	learnt/learned	learnt/learned
to leave	left	left
to lose	lost	lost
to make	made	made
to mean	meant	meant
to meet	met	met
to overtake	overtook	overtaken
to pay	paid	paid
to put	put	put
to re-sit	re-sat	re-sat
to ride	rode	ridden
to rise	rose	risen
to run	ran	run
to see	saw	seen
to set	set	set
to shoot	shot	shot
to sing	sang	sung
to sink	sank	sunk
to sit	sat	sat
to spend	spent	spent
to spread	spread	spread
to stand	stood	stood
to steal	stole	stolen
to sweep	swept	swept
to take	took	taken
to teach	taught	taught
to tell	told	told
to think	thought	thought
to throw	threw	thrown
to understand	understood	understood
to win	won	won
to write	wrote	written

Index

The words contained in the index appear in the first twelve chapters. The words in the Features chapter are not listed here.